S0-BCW-062

TREASURY
OF SPORTS HUMOR

Witty Stories and Anecdotes
from the World of Sports

By HERMAN L. MASIN

Editor,
SCHOLASTIC COACH

PRENTICE-HALL, INC.
Englewood Cliffs, N. J.

© 1960 BY

PRENTICE-HALL, INC.

ENGLEWOOD CLIFFS, N. J.

ALL RIGHTS RESERVED. NO PART OF THIS BOOK
MAY BE REPRODUCED IN ANY FORM, BY MIMEO-
GRAPH OR ANY OTHER MEANS, WITHOUT PER-
MISSION IN WRITING FROM THE PUBLISHER.

LIBRARY OF CONGRESS
CATALOG CARD NUMBER 60-16566

First printing .... September, 1960
Second printing .... March, 1961
Third printing .... July, 1962

PRINTED IN THE UNITED STATES OF AMERICA
93067—MO

TABLE OF CONTENTS

FROM THE BULLPEN

CONSIDERABLY less than four score and seven years ago—in 1954, to be exact—the writer brought forth into the coaching world a new volume conceived in humor and dedicated to the proposition that coaches and athletic directors needed a sourcebook that would lighten their ever-expanding speech-making load.

This book—the *Speaker's Treasury of Sport Stories* (Prentice-Hall, Inc.)—succeeded, not beyond the writer's wildest dreams, but adequately enough. So adequately, in fact, that a demand arose for a sequel.

And here it is—a brand new collection of the funniest sports rib-ticklers extant, amassed after five bloody years of collecting. Some of the anecdotes have appeared in *Scholastic Coach* Magazine's widely read "Coaches' Corner" department. Others appear for the first time. All of them have a dual purpose—to entertain the reader and to be converted to practical use by the speaker.

At one time or another, every coach is called upon for a speech, and there's nothing like a funny anecdote to warm up an audience and establish a nice rapport. The stories in this book provide a lot of this ham-munition for the coach-speaker.

Few of the anecdotes are sacrosanct; all of them can be changed in time, place and cast to fit the particular situation. That's one of the blessed oddities of the sports anecdote—the way it keeps getting switched and reshaped as it travels from mouth to mouth.

The writer lays no claim to the originality of these funny-boners. All of them have been culled from magazines, newspapers, and directly from the "horses'" mouths. To give credit where credit is due would be impossible. The list would run longer than Wilt Chamberlain's right arm.

But some acknowledgment is necessary; and the writer would like to tip his thin forelock respectfully to such nice people as: Herb Simons, editor of *Baseball Digest*; Dan Parker, sports editor of the New York *Daily Mirror*; Sam Molen, sports director of KMBC, Kansas City; Charlie Beck, staff artist for *Scholastic Magazines*; and the coaches by-lined under the various short pieces in the book.

H. L. M.

I

GRIDIRON GRINS

KEEP OFF THE GRASS

The Detroit Lions used to have a lot of fun with their five-by-five, 305-pound middle guard monster, Les Bingaman. One afternoon Bingaman was standing in the middle of the field, entranced by Bobby Layne's pin-point passing. Bobby, catching the little monster with his mouth open, broke the spell.

"Gee, move around, Bing," he drawled. "You're killing the grass."

HAPPY CHASE

After a week of intensive drilling on the practice field, Albie Bansavage, the ferocious Southern Cal linebacker, walked into his history class and was asked how the Constitution evolved.

Albie elaborated at great length, finishing with real linebacking gusto: "And we're all proud of our country's motto: 'Life, Liberty, and the Happiness of Pursuit!' "

MAN TALK

Interviewing the great Bear Bryant at the beginning of the season, the local sportscribe asked, "How many men do you have on your squad this year, Bear?"

"About half," snapped the Alabama mentor.

BAND STAND

At the Liberty Bowl game last year, Bear Bryant refused to be impressed by the Penn State band.

"Why, the Penn State band has 125 members!" he was told.

"So what?" drawled the Bear. "The Alabama band red-shirts that many every year."

TIGHT SQUEEZE

Like the proud boast made by Charlie Winner, backfield coach for the Baltimore Colts: "When Big Daddy Lipscomb puts on his uniform his pants are so tight that he's gotta take ether to take 'em off."

SON-SHINE

Before moving on to the Air Force Academy, Ben Martin had some lean years at Virginia. The Cavaliers were beaten badly one Saturday, and Ben asked his little son what he had thought of the game.

"Sir," the boy said, "You ain't much of a coach, are you?"

"The only thing I could say," shudders Ben in retrospect, "is 'Don't say ain't.'"

IMPROVISATION DELUXE

The teams were tied with two minutes to go when the coach sent his second-string qb in with a specific play. After looking over the defense, the scrub substituted a play of his own. It went for a td that won the game.

After congratulating the hero, the exhilarated coach asked him what prompted him to improvise.

"It was strictly a hunch," was the reply. "I looked at the halfback. His number was 6. Then I looked at the fullback. His number was 7. So I called play number 11."

"But that adds up to 13," gasped the startled mentor.

"Maybe so," responded the kid. "But if I was as smart as you, we wouldn't have won the game."

FRAN-TIC LINEMAN

When Fran Woidzik tried out for the Washington Redskins, his lumbering style of locomotion drew the ire of line coach Ernie Hefferle.

"Didn't you ever learn to run?" snapped Ernie.

The Buffalo rookie drew himself up, affixed a steely eye on his coach, and replied softly, "Where I come from, we stood still and fought."

PHILOSOPHY COURSE

The line coach of a professional football club was being interviewed for the head coaching job at an effete ivy college.

"What's your football philosophy?" queried the chairman of the athletic board.

"To explode across the line and rip out the opponents' guts," gritted the hard-nose.

The chairman looked shocked. "Do you mean that literally?" he asked.

"Hell, no!" replied the coach. "I mean that physically."

THE COACH AT BAY

Walking off the field after watching his team fail to cross midfield all afternoon, the gloomy coach accidentally knocked down an old lady. Helping his victim to her feet, the coach contritely apologized, "I'm very sorry madam, no offense intended."

To which the lady snarled, "You're telling me!"

HIGH KICKERS

After Monty Sickles kicked his fifth field goal during the

1959 season, a reporter asked Notre Dame's A. D., Moose Krause, if Monty wasn't the greatest kicker South Bend ever had. Moose pondered the query, then said:

"No, I'd have to take our alumni."

SOMETHING TO CHEW ON

During spring training at West Virginia, a visitor approached Coach Art Lewis and kiddingly observed, "Gaining weight, aren't you, Pappy?"

"Sure am," drawled Pappy, "I want the alumni to have something to chew on this fall."

SHORT COUNT

Looking around at all the famous coaches milling in the lobby of the Hotel Astor, the smug Big Ten mentor turned to Harry Grayson, the NEA sports editor.

"How many great coaches do you think there are in this room?" he asked.

Harry surveyed him silently for a moment, then replied, "One less than you think."

MISSING IDENTIFICATION TAG

Jan Murray, the famous comedian, while emceeing a banquet, noted Charley Conerly, the Giants qb, seated at a front table.

"Oh, hello there, Chuck," he breezed. "Sorry I didn't notice you before. I didn't recognize you without Big Daddy Lipscomb sitting on you."

SWEET SMELL OF SUCCESS

The 1950 Colts had a center named Joel Williams, reports John Steadman. At a practice session, Coach Clem Crowe walked into a huddle and was almost overcome by an alcoholic breath.

"My God," Crowe cried, "not so early in the morning!"

"No, Coach," spoke up Williams. "That's from last night."

PARKER ROLLED

When Jim Parker came out of Ohio State to join the Colts, Coach Ewbank instructed Gino Marchetti to subject Jim to the acid test. Marchetti went around him. Then he'd pull Parker back and thunder on past. Finally, after doing everything but jump over him—he did that, too.

Parker was now completely bewildered. He nudged the opposing tackle, Artie Donovan. "Hey, Artie, what do I do now?"

"Shucks, Jim, if I were you, I'd applaud."

BACK TALK WANTED

Buddy Young provided much hilarity in his years with the Colts. One night in camp, Barney Poole cornered a bat and decided to put it in Buddy's room. But someone tipped off the chunky scatback, who quickly bolted his door. Poole banged on the portal and shouted, "Come on, Buddy, open up. I got something for you."

"Yeah, I know what you got," Young hollered back. "And you can keep it. I don't want nothing in my room that can't talk to me."

CIRCLING THE SQUARE-OFF

The Colts and Eagles met in a pre-season game and became involved in a dispute. When the boys started squaring off, Norm Van Brocklin, the Eagle qb, walked over to the enormous and very tough Colt end, Don Joyce.

"Listen, Champ," he said, "if a fight starts, remember, I'm on your side."

THE BISHOP'S MOVE

George Wright, Baylor sports news director, has been wowing the banquet circuit with the one about the bishop and the football coach arriving simultaneously at the pearly gates. The bishop is practically ignored, while the coach is greeted with a wild parade.

The bishop is kind of nonplussed. "If you do that for a football coach," he asked, "what do you do for a bishop?"

"Nothing," replies the guardian of the gates. "We get a bishop a week, but that's the first football coach we've ever had."

JOCKEYED SHORTS

Perhaps the best-received speech in Texas last year was Blackie Sherrod's short welcoming address at a Texas Hall of Fame luncheon. Quoth the Dallas *Times Herald* sports columnist:

"I am indeed grateful for this opportunity to rise and welcome you, particularly since I have always admired greatly the men being inducted into the Hall of Fame . . . since two great teams, Syracuse and Texas, are present . . . and also since the program is long and this is the last chance I'll have to straighten my shorts . . ."

BED CHECK

With all three of his qbs out of commission, Joe Kuharich, then coach of the Redskins, gathered his squad together on the day before the big game against the 49'ers.

"Let's face the facts, men," he said. "All we have available at qb tomorrow are two rookies—Don Bailey and Fred Wyant. We'll have to grind out the yards the hard way by rushing because our passing is null and void."

At curfew time that night, the routine room check was made by the assistant coach, Mike Nixon. Mike roamed up and down the corridors until he came to the room in which Bailey and Wyant were lodged.

"Everyone in bed?" sang out Mike into the darkness.

"We're here, Coach," replied a sleepy voice. "Both Null and Void."

UNCONDITIONED REFLEXES

Like the immortal Babe Ruth, that marvel of the gridiron, Bobby Layne, is famous for his disregard of the training rules. After coming to the Steelers, he once took a teammate on a tour of the bright lights and kept him out until practically game time.

Bobby walked into the dressing room, slipped into uniform, ducked his head under the cold water, and went out and promptly started bedazzling the enemy with his passing and running.

His companion of the evening, however, could barely move. After five minutes on the field, he collapsed. Layne walked over to him, looked down, and clucked his tongue.

"The trouble with you, buddy," he drawled, "is that you're just not in condition."

AMBIDEXTROUS WIT

Navy's 235-pound destroyer, Bob Reifsnyder, was as quick with an answer as he was on his feet. During a blackboard drill in preparation for the 1957 California game, a scout was briefing the Middies on the Cal personnel.

"You gotta watch that California quarterback," he said. "He's dangerous. He's ambidextrous."

Reifsnyder started to laugh. The scout looked at him and said, "What are you laughing at, you big lug? I bet you don't even know what ambidextrous means."

"The heck I don't," snapped Bob. "It means he runs with both feet."

FISH AND TACKLE

The big Navy tackle was a blasting fullback at Baldwin (N.Y.) High. When he entered the Naval Academy, Coach Eddie Erdelatz took one look at him and said, "This fellow's got to play tackle. I can't afford the luxury of a 230-pound fullback."

How did Bob like switching from fullback to tackle? "The first thing you notice is that the other guys are right smack in front of you. They look bigger, tougher, and *sooner!*"

HIGH SOCIETY

Reifsnyder was tossed out of three games for fisticuffs. When Navy took the field against Rice in the Cotton Bowl game, the Owl quarterback, King Hill, quipped, "Hey, Reifsnyder, I understand you're a member of the Left Jab and Right Cross Society."

Quick-witted Bob snapped right back, "I'm a member, all right, but not in good standing."

THE BEAR WENT OVER THE MOUNTAIN

The Middle East situation was reaching a climax while the coaching clinic was in session. One afternoon Bear Bryant,

Alabama's head man and a recruiter without peer, asked the clinic director how the situation was developing in Lebanon.

"I suppose you're worried because you've got some big tackle you're recruiting in Beirut," kidded the director.

"I'd recruit in Moscow if I could find a prospect there," retorted the Bear.

THE MO THE MERRIER

Dick (Little Mo) Modzelewski, the pro Giants' ferocious tackle, was bragging about the family brawn. Dick cited his brother Ed (Big Mo), the Browns' fullback, and up-and-coming Eugene, a 14-year-old 205-pound high school prodigy who's called "Dyna Mo."

"Yeah," interrupted Kyle Rote. "And after him there ain't no Mo."

LIGHT-HEARTED STORY

The near-sighted pro coach was rapidly losing his temper at his first skull session. "You at the back of the room," he roared, "what's the left tackle's assignment on the fullback counter up the middle?"

"I don't know."

"Well, then, can you tell me what the right end does on the halfback run-pass option?"

"I don't know."

"I taught that only yesterday," the coach bellowed. "What were you doing at the time?"

"I was out drinking beer with some friends."

The coach turned purple. "You have the audacity to stand there and tell me that! How do you expect to make the team?"

"Hell, Coach, I don't. I'm an electrician, and I just came in here to fix the lights."

THINK AGAIN

Kink Richards was a rookie halfback for the N. Y. Giants back in 1933, the year the pros returned the goal posts to the goal line. Against the Eagles that season, Richards broke loose and appeared sure to score but suddenly set the ball down on the 5-yard line. He had forgotten about the shift of the goal posts and thought he was in the end zone.

Richards tried to explain to Coach Steve Owen. He began, "I thought . . ."

"Never mind thinking!" bellowed Owen. "It slows down the offense!"

The sequel to this outburst came later. The next time Richards had trouble on the field, he was ready for Owen. As he trotted to the bench, he yelled: "Coach, don't say a word. I was thinking again!"

A FINE IDEA

Tom Thorpe, the famous referee, once suspected that a lineman was swinging fists at his opponent. But he always looked too late to see the blow. The opponent finally rebelled. With no subterfuge whatever, he simply reached up and clobbered the dirty-playing lineman.

The original culprit howled to Thorpe. But he received no satisfaction. "I sure did see it," snapped Thorpe. "And I thought it was a good idea."

OUT IN THE COLT

Jack Lavelle, the late great N. Y. Giants scout, after scouting the Colts in Baltimore: "I'm glad we don't have to play the Colt fans. They're tougher than the team."

BLISTERS UNDER THE SKIN

A wry commentary on second guessers by North Carolina coach Jim Tatum: "When I go to bed after losing a game and lie there wondering why I didn't pass or kick or run under such a condition, why, I know that 20,000 other people are in their beds wondering about just that very thing, too. I tell you it's a great feeling of fellowship."

YOU CAN GET KILT!

After Iowa slaughtered California in the 1959 Rose Bowl game, Bob Hunter of the Los Angeles *Examiner* cracked, "Even the players in Iowa's Scottish bagpipe band scored a decisive triumph over the Golden Bears. They 'kilt' them, too."

POOL OF PRAISE

In presenting a gift to 1958 Coach-of-the-Year Paul Dietzel, the toastmaster of the Louisiana State annual banquet averred that "We're not giving you a new car because too many coaches have used them to drive away. We're giving you something you can't move—a swimming pool for your backyard."

WELL, ALL RIGHT!

A Pittsburgh fan fighting his way into Pitt Stadium for the Oklahoma-Pittsburgh game charged into three fellows wearing jackets bearing the letters, "OU". Having read all about those fabulous Oklahoma oil men, the Pitt fan yelled, "I'll bet you two oil wells on the game."

One of the Oklahoma men gave him a bored look, then slowly went through each of his pockets. "Sorry," he finally drawled, "but I haven't any small change with me."

MATING CALL

Charming and wise are precisely the words for Mrs. Ann Hayes, wife of Woody of Ohio State football fame. One day she picked up the phone and heard a voice say, "Your husband is a fathead!"

"What husband isn't?" she sweetly replied.

THE HELL OF IT

The angels in heaven were kibitzing with the devils down below. "If we ever played a football game, we'd murder you," they jockeyed. "After all, we have all the All-Americans up here in heaven."

"So what?" sneered the devils. "We have all the great coaches."

FOR PETE'S SAKE

That man, Pete Carlesimo, head football coach at Scranton U., is an after-dinner speaker without peer. We heard him for the first time at a writers' luncheon, and our sides are still sore. For 20 minutes, he panicked the scribes with an hilarious run of dry wit.

"Gentlemen," he started, "I've been introduced as the head football coach at Scranton. Well, I want you to know that in addition to that I'm director of athletics. I'm also director of physical education. And in addition to those three jobs, I run two cafeterias. But the good Jesuit brothers

I work for aren't unappreciative. If I continue to do a good job, they've promised to put me on full time.

"When I played for Jim Crowley at Fordham, they accused the football team of never going to classes. That's a lie. Why, every single day on the way to practice we passed a classroom and looked inside. They had nice blackboards and seats and everything.

"One Saturday we played SMU and were we outclassed. They had been taught all the fundamentals of offense and defense plus a beautiful six-inch uppercut. How could we play 'em even when all we'd been taught was a four-inch uppercut?

"I think Buff Donelli is one of the greatest coaches in the country. I'm not saying that because he's Italian—but because I am.

"People accuse me of being partial to Italians just because my team speaks Italian in the huddle. I assure you they do so purely for cultural purposes.

"Why, I married a nice Irish girl—because I thought she was Italian. Our union has been blessed with seven beautiful children—four are fair and blonde, the other three are dark. My wife washes the dark kids with chlorox, while I wash the blonde kids with olive oil."

The man goes on and on and on in this extremely funny way.

PLANE SPEAKING

The plane carrying the Pittsburgh football team to its 1958 date with UCLA developed engine trouble and eventually had to set down at Albuquerque. But the players never lost their composure.

"Coach Michelosen is going back to the single wing," one

player cracked. Another quipped, "The season hasn't even begun and our new offense is sputtering already."

BY HOOK OR CROOK

When "Crazy Legs" Hirsh once made a good-will tour of a prison, an inmate who coached the prison football team told him he had worked out the greatest play ever devised.

Hirsh looked at the diagram. "It's pretty good," he admitted, "except for one thing: You have five men in the backfield. That's illegal."

"I know," confessed the coach. "But you know us: we cheat."

LONESOME END

Jack Lavelle, the late scout, was explaining Army's dynamic new lonesome end to ex-Notre Dame coach, Terry Brennan.

"What happens to the lonesome end when the trainer comes out with the water bucket?" asked Terry. "Does he go over for a drink?"

"No, siree," flipped Lavelle. "He sticks his hand into his pocket and whips out some K rations."

SEMANTIC ANTIC

Gonzaga U.'s importation of 7 ft. 3½ in. Jean Claude Lefebvre from France recalls the football coach who discovered a titanic 250-lb. youth in the wilds of Argentina. He brought him home and registered him at the university, getting him a special tutor for English.

About a week later the coach looked up the kid and asked him how he was getting along. "I know the English good," the boy replied. "I can even say 'Come here' and the person will understand."

"But suppose you want a person to go there," replied the coach. "What do you do?"

The wild bull pondered a moment. "Well," he finally answered, "I go over there and then say, 'Come here.'"

HE CHOKED UP

The rough, tough tackle came running off the field. "What's the matter with you?" exclaimed the coach.

"The ref just threw me out of the game," he said.

"What for?"

"I dunno."

So the coach, the next time-out, beckoned to the official. "What did you toss out Zippo for?" he asked.

"Because I caught him choking the opposing quarterback," the official snapped.

The coach was nonplussed. But just for a moment. "Ah, you didn't have to get mad," he grinned. "The kid is just a practical choker."

CHRIS-CROSS

Chris Shenkel, the pet football telecaster of CBS, seems to be a nice enough chap and owns a nice enough voice. But he has two difficulties: (1) he doesn't know much football, and (2) he exhibits an odd sort of inarticularity.

Before turning the dial after the first quarter of the Montclair-Bloomfield (N.J.) schoolboy game in 1957, we caught these weirdies:

"Haines gains yards on the play, but is stopped in his tracks."

"No official state crown is awarded (in New Jersey), but mythically is talked about."

"They're playing like an underdog—with renewed courage."

"The penalty is against Montclair." (While the officials and the teams are trotting down the field to change sides after the quarter.)

This fellow Schenkel is carrying on in the glorious tradition of Graham McNamee and Harry Wismer.

NUTS TO YOU

A well-known football coach visited a psycho ward to talk football with the patients just a few hours after his team blew a 14-point lead in the last quarter. In the middle of his talk, one of the patients broke in with: "Ah, you're a bum. All you do is blow leads."

The ward doctor apologized to the coach. "It's very embarrassing," he said. "But you know: It's the first sensible thing he's said in months."

DESTINATION UNKNOWN

1957 was an awfully bumpy year for Coach Ed Doherty of Arizona. But he held on tightly to his sense of humor. At a Booster Club luncheon he was asked rather pointedly what he planned to do after his retirement from coaching.

"I'm going to tuck a football under my arm and head south of the border," he wryly replied. "When I get far enough south for someone to ask, 'What's that thing you're carrying?', that's where I'm going to settle down!"

BUMP ON THE HEAD

Another coach who had it real rough in 1957 was Acting Coach Bob Hicks of Indiana. The poor Hoosiers were walloped by some astronomical scores. Against Minnesota, an Indiana lineman was shaken up and removed from the game. A bit groggy, he was asked the usual simple questions to determine his condition.

One such query was, "What's the score of the game?", then 7-0 in favor of Minnesota.

"We're three touchdowns ahead," replied the lineman.

Coach Hicks instantly turned to the bench. "Please," he implored, "somebody hit me on the head, too!"

A WIRE FROM THE WISE

Pressure-plagued though he is, Michigan State's Duffy Daugherty always has a witty winner on the tip of his tongue. Before last season's homecoming game against Illinois, he claims he got this wire from an alumnus:

"Remember, Coach, we're all behind you—win or tie."

SEANCE, SAY UNCLE!

During a skull session at a football clinic, a group of coaches thought it would be a nice gesture to let one of their recently departed brethren know how much they missed him. So they set up a seance around a large magnetic diagram board on which were diagrammed the latest trends in offensive football.

"Bud, Bud," intoned the medium. "Can you hear us?"

No answer. So the medium tried again. "Bud, Bud, can you hear us?"

Finally, out of the great void into the darkened room a thin voice was heard:

"Sorry, fellers, I'm not interested. I'm a defensive coach."

VOICE OF INEXPERIENCE

The newly appointed 22-year-old head coach of a small

college was attending his first annual meeting of the American Football Coaches Assn. His old college mentor took him aside.

"Look, Bill," he advised. "You're going to be nervous at first. You'll be overawed by all the great coaches you're going to meet. But don't let it get you down. The first day you're here, you'll wonder how you made it. After that, you'll wonder how the rest of us made it."

ASSISTANT COACH

Ohio State's great fullback, Bob White, is an extremely versatile gent who can do just about everything on a football field. Against Michigan in 1957, he had a great day playing offensive center, defensive center, offensive fullback and defensive fullback. Late in the game, Coach Woody Hayes pulled him out for a breather. As White trotted off the field, a reporter in the press box remarked:

"Look at White. He's played offensive center, defensive center, offensive fullback, and defensive fullback. Now Hayes is taking him out to help him coach."

QUEENLY BEARING

Maryland's governor, Theodore McKeldin, played host to Queen Elizabeth and Prince Philip at the Maryland-North Carolina football game in 1957.

The Queen's first question when the teams thundered onto the field was: "Where do you get all those enormous players?"

"Your majesty," replied the governor, "that's a very embarrassing question."

LITTLE BOY EDDIE

Back in the days of Eddie LeBaron, the College of the

Pacific football team was walking through a train en route to the diner when they passed two elderly women.

"Who are all those big men?" one little old lady said to the other.

"Oh," replied the latter, "that's the College of the Pacific football team."

"My," the first lady said, looking at LeBaron, "isn't that nice. One of them is taking his little boy to the game."

POOR LITTLE BIG DADDY

People are always asking little Eddie LeBaron if pro football is dirty. "No," he always answers. "You have to remember that a fellow like Big Daddy Lipscomb has to defend himself. After all, he's only 6-feet-5 and weighs just 290 pounds."

THE THIRD LICK

Though a deeply religious person, the football coach also was something of a realist. Before the big game against his rough, tough traditional rival, he gathered his squad around him and warned them about the rough stuff the opponents would throw at them.

"Now, fellers," he said, "the Good Book tells us that if an enemy smacks you on the cheek, that's all right. Turn your other cheek. And if the opponents smack that cheek, too, it's still all right. But, gentlemen, the third lick—*the third lick, I say, belongs to you!*"

GENIE-OLOGY

Sitting in his office one evening, the tired football coach heard a clap of thunder. He looked up and there was a genie. "What are you doing here?" the coach asked.

"I came to grant you a wish. Is there anything special you want?"

"And how!" murmured the coach. "Boy, could the wife and I use a two-month vacation in Bermuda."

"It's all yours."

"But who'll run the team while I'm gone?"

"I will," replied the genie.

Next morning the coach and his wife were reclining in Bermuda while the genie was sitting at the coach's desk. In walked the equipment manager. The genie explained that he was taking over for the coach. "What can I do for you?"

The equipment manager sneered. "What can you do for me? Huh, make me a dozen rubber sideline parkas."

"Okay," said the genie. "You ARE a dozen rubber sideline parkas!"

CALIFORNIA, HERE I COME!

Red Sanders admitted he could never feel like a native Californian. "But I can feel like an average Californian," he would add. "I've been hit three times by a car, have had the virus twice, and owe $24,000."

CHAPPED LIVER

Bear Bryant had a rugged boyhood and it's still hard for him to understand how a minor injury can keep a boy out of a football game. Queried on the condition of one of his squads shortly after he became a head coach, he sarcastically snapped, "We're in pretty good shape—except one of our boys has chapped lips."

IN MARBLE HALLS

The young football coach, handicapped by speech difficulties, returned to his alma mater and looked up the chairman of the speech department. "Professor Higgins," he said, "could you tell me how to become a good public speaker?"

"I've got a special course for football coaches," answered the prof. "All you have to do is practice for a while with pebbles in your mouth."

So the young football coach began practicing with a mouthful of marbles. Every day he reduced the number by one. He became a public speaker when he had lost all his marbles.

A GOOD MATCH

After winning a big game in the Cotton Bowl, the visiting coach was given a big dinner at a downtown hotel. He proved insufferable with his boasting.

"I'm a self-made man," he bragged. "I was a high school coach, then a principal. Now I'm a big time football coach and have $100,000 in the bank."

A nearby Texan quietly looked him up and down. "All right, son," he drawled, "I'll match you for it."

PIE IN THE SKY

Flying East for a ball game one Friday, Joe Kuharich turned down a steak dinner. He explained to a sportswriting friend that as a Roman Catholic he couldn't eat meat on Friday.

"I'm eating mine," his friend replied, "and I'm also a Catholic. I've heard there's an automatic dispensation when you're in a plane and they're only serving meat."

"It may be so," answered Kuharich. "But we're a little too close to headquarters up here."

HOME ON THE COUCH

The slave-driving coach, dismayed at his failure, decided

to go to a psychiatrist. He stretched out on the couch and began mumbling his troubles.

At a crucial point, the psychiatrist missed some words and asked: "Would you mind repeating what you just said?"

"I said," roared the coach, "for some reason nobody seems to like me. Why don't you pay attention, you knucklehead?"

POSITIVELY THINKING

The new coach was one of those fiends for psychology. In his first skull session, he harped on confidence, the power of positive thinking, and self-mesmerization.

"You can improve yourself if you improve your thoughts," he said earnestly. "You *are* what you *think*!"

Whereupon a tackle nudged a guard. "If that's true," he whispered, "I'm either Jayne Mansfield or a Cadillac!"

SPAGHETTI HUDDLE

Back in his days at Maryland, Jim Tatum was driven mad by a butter-fingered quarterback who cost him at least three ball games. After the season ended, Big Jim was having dinner in a local restaurant when a waiter dropped a mess of spaghetti down his neck.

"Oh, excuse me, sir," mumbled the waiter; then, looking at Tatum closely, his face lit up in recognition. "Say, Mr. Tatum," he exclaimed, "I have a relative who plays for you."

"Don't go any further," groaned Tatum. "From the way you handled that spaghetti, I know exactly who you mean."

IT'S NOT ALL GREEK

Two Greek immigrants were watching their first football game. After a few minutes of mystified silence, one turned to the other and said, "This is all American to me."

THEM DRY BONES!

Definitely one of football's nicer guys, Duffy Daugherty possesses a sharp turn of phrase that puts him in great demand on the limp-chicken-and-fruit-cocktail circuit. His pungent oratory is neatly exemplified in one of his recent talks on the qualities he looks for as a football coach:

"Of course, we like them big at Michigan State. But we'll settle for players with three kinds of bones—a funny bone, a wishbone, and a backbone. The funnybone is to enjoy a laugh, even at one's own expense. The wishbone is to think big, set one's goals high and to have dreams and ambitions.

"And the backbone—well, that's what a boy needs to get up and go to work and make all those dreams come true."

THE NUMBERS RACKET

The ambitious young college coach, out to build a rep, recruited a herd of young oxen from the backwoods who, though tremendously built, had had little schooling and no football experience.

At his first skull session, he used a blackboard to explain his entire system, chalking in one play after another. His oxen looked at him blankly. The coach continued, chalking, erasing, chalking. Finally, he noticed his biggest and dullest recruit watching him intently.

"Abner," he exclaimed happily, "I'm sure you'd like to ask some questions."

"Yah, sure, Coach," drawled the hillbilly. "Where do them numbers go when you rub 'em off the board?"

PAST BALL

The veteran coach was giving advice to his young successor: "Be careful what you say to newspapermen. If you don't, someday they'll dig up something you said in the past, compare it with something you just said, then claim you're a liar."

"Coach," said the youngster, "have they ever claimed that on you?"

"Heck, no," replied the coach, "they proved it."

THAT'S ENTERTAINMENT

Which recalls the one about the wily old egotistical coach who could always extricate himself from an embarrassing predicament. When the T-formation mushroomed into popularity in 1940, he declared that it was a passing fancy; that it didn't stand a chance of catching hold and enduring.

About 17 years later, a local scribe came across this quote in the "morgue" and just to needle the coach, brought it up at a downtown quarterbacks' luncheon. Everyone snickered as the scribe reeled off the ancient quote.

But the veteran mentor still carried the day. "Gentlemen," he said, rising to his feet, "I'd like to say that I find it incredible that a coach as intelligent as I could ever have entertained such a notion."

THE BUTTS OF ALL HUMOR

One of the country's brightest columnists, Fred Russell of the *Nashville Banner,* has compounded the wit and wisdom of 30 years of sportswriting into *Bury Me in an Old Press Box* (A. S. Barnes & Co.). Several of the outstanding rib-ticklers therein follow:

Characteristic of Wally Butt's homespun humor are his tales of woe, deprecating his team's (Georgia) chances. One time between halves of a spring intrasquad game, he told Russell not to go away, that he was going to try something new the second half:

"I'm going to line up the linemen back to back, instead of face to face, and see if they block any better."

Wally once complained that he needed to get a team manicurist because his players were making so many finger-nail tackles!

AN OLD-FASHIONED

When it was suggested that his single-wing offense might be old-fashioned, the late Red Sanders replied: "Maybe it's a horse-and-buggy offense, but I like to think we have a TV set on the dashboard."

DEVIL-MAY-CARE SPIRIT

At his very first meeting with the UCLA squad, Red Sanders told the players he was new on the scene, that UCLA was a mighty big place, that he couldn't check on them closely, and that he had been told that if a boy was so inclined, he could get into devilment right on the campus.

With that a big tackle raised his hand and asked, "Where?"

BLOOD AND SANDERS

Red Sanders never kidded himself about the hazards of coaching. When a cheering horde of students serenaded his apartment, pleading for him to stay at UCLA instead of accepting a U. of Florida offer, he told them: "No coach in the world is worth all this excitement." But aside to his wife, he muttered, "Which one has the rope?"

ACID TONGUE SANDWICH

The acid-tongued coach couldn't stand the referee's fumbl-

ing any longer. As the official passed the bench, he bellowed,
"Open your eyes, stupid, you're missing a great game!"

CHARLOTTE RUSE

George Ratterman, former quarterback for the Browns, was
never accused of being slow-witted. Sent in against the Bears
one afternoon, he was just about to take the pass from center
when he spied his old Notre Dame buddy, George Connor,
across the line.

"How are you, George?" he yelled, lifting his head.

Connor grinned, stood up, and shouted right back, "Hi,
George!"—then swore as Ratterman quickly ran a play
through him for 20 yards!

GIRL CRAZY

The athletic staff of Iowa State Teachers was discussing
the merits of having their children engaged in athletics.
"Frankly," commented backfield coach Ed Lyons, "I hope
none of my kids ever play football. In fact, I'm going to
discourage it."

The other coaches looked at him in dismay until they
remembered—Lyons is the father of six daughters.

BIG PITCH

According to "informed" sources, the U. of Houston made
a tremendous pitch for Bud Wilkinson one winter. Some
Houston tycoon was supposed to have offered him an oil
well and an ocean-going yacht. When Wilkinson said no,
the bid was supposedly expanded to two oil wells and two
yachts, one of them air-conditioned.

This was too much for Red Smith, the sharp-witted sports
columnist. "Can you picture Wilkinson getting the news?"

he wrote. "Air conditioning in only one yacht? Who's supposed to sweat it out in the cheap yacht—the line coach?"

FORMATION RIGHT!

Pappy Waldorf may have lost his job at California in 1956, but he certainly retained his sense of humor. During a filming of the California-UCLA game, in which the Uclans scored five touchdowns, Pappy remarked, "This was our most popular formation this season."

The picture showed California lined up to receive the kickoff!

A GOOD START

With Coach Frank Leahy confined to a sick bed, Moose Krause took over the squad and delivered a fiery pep talk. All worked up, he shouted, "Come on, men, let's go out there and get 'em!"

Nobody moved. The Moose looked at the squad unbelievingly. "Coach," explained one of the boys, "you haven't named the starting lineup."

"Hell!" roared Moose, "We'll all start!"

ON THE BALL

Upon arriving at Iowa City with his UCLA eleven, Red Sanders scheduled a workout the day before the game. As the players lined up, the student manager approached Red. "Coach," he said embarrassedly, "I remembered everything on the trip—except the footballs."

Sanders looked at him blankly, then said with withering softness, "That's all right, son. Just get the Iowa coach on the phone and see if we can change this thing to a track meet."

TAPPED OUT

A coach at the 1956 coaches' convention was explaining his team's 40 point defeat in one of its big games. "It was due almost entirely to the way our center handed the ball back to our quarterback."

That was too much for Fred Russell of the *Nashville Banner.* "That's like blaming the Johnstown flood on a leaky faucet in Altoona, Pa.," he cracked.

DUMMIES BY THE DOZEN

The most enterprising soul at the covention was an inventor who said he was mass-producing dummies for students who want to hang their coach in effigy. He expected a landslide business in September, October, and November.

THE BEAST AND THE BEAR

He was 6 ft. 5 in., weighed 255 lbs., had a blue-black beard, and looked like the toughest, meanest hombre alive. He showed up on an eastern college campus the second week of pre-season football practice and wanted to know if they could use him. The coach had him in a uniform in two seconds flat. He put him in with the second team on defense.

On the first play, the big boy knocked the offensive tackle unconscious, grabbed the ball-carrier by the arm, and tossed him for a 25-yard loss. On the second play, he picked up an offensive guard, hurled him against the blocking back, stiff-armed another back into oblivion, picked up the would-be passer and hurled him to earth 15 yards to the rear. On the third play, he tore an awesome hole into the offensive line, sent two blocking backs reeling, thundered into the kicker, rapped him unconscious, picked up the ball and carried it over the goal line—with six offensive players on his back.

The coach, startled and gleeful, yanked him off the field. "Son," he said, "you're the type of student we like at dear old Harfard. I'm hereby offering you a four-year scholarship. By the way, where do you come from?"

"Birmingham, Alabama," growled the fearsome beast.

"Gosh, how did Bear Bryant ever let you get away?" queried the coach.

"Because he thought I was too damned effeminate," snarled the animal.

TV SPECTACULAR

Wisconsin football coach Milt Bruhn explained his 9-7 upset of Michigan State in 1958 by saying, "With a national TV audience we had to put on a better show than we did against Iowa on regional TV."

Which led communications tycoon Earl Gammons to observe, "Even the football coaches must watch their national ratings."

DISNEYLAND

For the past 10 years or so, the Oklahoma Sooners have been making mince meat out of the Big Seven Conference. When the Big Seven took on an eighth member in 1957 (Oklahoma State), the *Kansas City Star* asked its readers to suggest a new name for the Conference.

The prize suggestion came from columnist Bill Vaughan. It was: "Oklahoma and the Seven Dwarfs."

CHALK TALK

The practice field was across the highway from the locker rooms, and every afternoon the players would have to cross the road after donning their gear. The school, fearful of their gridders' safety, put up a sign for motorists: "Drive carefully. Don't injure our players."

Under which a discontented fan chalked: "Wait for the Coach!"

TRIPLE-TALKER

Upon returning home after making his first after-dinner speech, the coach was accosted by his ever-loving spouse. "How was your talk tonight, dear?" she asked.

"Which one?" groaned the coach. "The one I was going to give? The one I did give? Or the one I delivered so brilliantly to myself on the way home in the car?"

GUARD ALMIGHTY

Guards are defined as "fullbacks with their brains knocked out." And this pro guard fitted the description to a T. One day he was knocked cold and had to be sent to the hospital. A few days later, a reporter asked the coach, "Did old Jim come out okay?"

"No," replied the coach, "he didn't come out all right. He's back just the way he used to be."

SWEETS FOR ROSY

Watching Rosy Grier, 290-pound tackle of the N. Y. Giants, demolishing the enemy with his bare hands, Steve Lieser, the Los Angeles granite and marble super salesman, shook his head in amazement. "What a monster!" he ejaculated.

His friend grinned. "What would you do if you met him in a dark alley?"

Steve thought a while, then said gravely, "I'd feed him candy."

HOLY PETE!

Army's great All-American, Pete Dawkins, exemplified class on all counts—as athlete, scholar, personality boy, leader, and citizen. So exalted was his reputation that the other cadets took to inventing tales of his ability to do anything.

There's the story that Bill Carpenter, on hearing that he had been named to succeed Dawkins as football captain, climbed to the top of the nearby reservoir and began removing his shoes.

"What are you doing?" asked the amazed reservoir warden.

"They want me to follow in Pete's footsteps," replied Bill. "So I have to learn how to walk on water."

CAN'T SINK THE ARMY

Dale Hall, the Army's new coach, scouts this story. He took Dawkins up to the reservoir and dropped him into a 40-foot depth. And it turned out that Pete couldn't walk on water after all.

"He sank right up to his knees," the coach alleged.

DEMORALIZING MOOD

Like the wry but trenchant way in which Al Davis, assistant coach at U.S.C., describes the idea of defensive pursuit. "To demoralize the ball-carrier, we want 11 men to reach the ball in the minimum amount of time, all arriving in a bad mood."

MAN ALIVE

After the Detroit Lions finished the 1958 season, a sportswriter cornered Jim David, the doughty little defensive back, in the locker room.

"Would you say you had a good season?" the scribe asked.

"Any time you come out of a pro season alive, you've had a good year," grinned the little fellow.

DE LUXE WRAPPER

One day the Baltimore Colt coach, Weeb Ewbank, asked "Big Daddy" Lipscomb how come he was such a marvelous tackler.

"Coach," grunted the behemoth tackle, "I just wrap my arms around the whole backfield and peel 'em off one by one until I get to the ball-carrier. Him I keep."

KEEPING POSTED

The Bears and 49'ers were having one of their typical Pier 6 brawls, when Joe "The Jet" Perry took the ball, put his head down, tore through a big hole, and rammed head-first into the goal post.

The 49'ers toughie bounced off the post, wobbled a bit, and flopped over for a touchdown. The 49'ers went into a huddle for the extra-point. But there was no Perry. Finally he staggered into the huddle. He blinked a few times, shook his head, and looked at his teammates.

"You, Bob (St. Clair), you got your man. But which of you so-and-sos missed the block on that linebacker?"

MASTERMIND OVER MATTER

Duffy Daugherty, Michigan State football coach: "They tell me some of our freshmen look awfully good. But they're probably not ready for the varsity as yet. Remember, they haven't had the benefit of my coaching yet."

MOTION DENIED!

Earle Edwards, North Carolina State coach: "I made two suggestions to the rules committee, and neither was accepted. I asked that the goal line be moved nearer my team and the fourth quarter be eliminated."

STANDS TO REASON

An American student was explaining the game of football to a foreign exchange student. "There are two ends, two tackles, two guards, a center, one fullback, two halfbacks, and 75,001 quarterbacks."

"75,001 quarterbacks?" queried the foreigner in astonishment.

"Yeah," explained the American, "one on the field and 75,000 up in the stands."

SNAKE-HIPS

Indiana's football coach, Phil Dickens, couldn't help but be impressed by a glowing letter from an ex-Hoosier star extolling a high school prospect.

"He's lean and mean," the letter ran, "and in the summer he hunts rattlesnakes for 50¢ a pound."

PRAISED BY THE LORD

Forest Evashevski's housekeeper at Iowa is devoutly religious. After a Rose Bowl victory, Hawkeye fans presented

Ev with a new car. He drove it home, pulled up in front
of his house, and strolled to the front porch.

"What do you think?" Ev asked the housekeeper.

The good woman appraised him silently, then said, "Just
remember, the same people who praised Jesus also crucified
him."

GAY DECEIVER

Bob Hope claims he played football in school. "I was
known as Neckline Hope. I was always plunging down the
middle, but never really showing anything."

SMALL FRY

The football coach was explaining how he sprang the upset
of the season with a team averaging 105 pounds. "My line
wasn't big enough to open holes for my big backs to run
through. So I figured if we're opening teenie-weenie holes,
why not use teenie-weenie backs to run through those
teenie-weenie holes? So I substituted my 4 by 6's, and it
worked. We scored three td's without a back over 6 inches
wide and 4 inches thick. I measured 'em. It was a perfect
fit."

THE GROSSCUP THAT CHEERS

Quick-witted Cactus Jack Curtice rocked the All-American
Football Clinic at Santa Barbara, Calif., while narrating a
1957 Utah film showing his quarterback, Lee Grosscup,
hitting on one spectacular pass after another.

"That Grosscup can throw long or short, hard or soft,"
raved the new Stanford coach. "Boy, is he going to miss me
this year!"

EXCESS BAGGAGE

Probably the funniest guy this side of Bob Hope, Cactus Jack Curtice is a raconteur without peer. His Tennessee Ernie delivery conceals a rapier wit and devastating sense of humor. Sample:

"Lots of people ask me how I stayed in coachin' all these years—bein' so stupid and all, I mean. Well, I'll tell you. Down in Texas one year, I got the biggest, tallest, and strongest two boys I could find. Then I gave each one of them the kind of scholarships you get at colleges down in Texas but not at Stanford—and I told these boys they had to do only one thing: after we lost a game, they had to hoist me up on their shoulders and carry me off the field.

"The folks would see that and they'd say, 'Oh, hell, ole Jack ain't much of a coach, but you can see the kids love him.' "

THEY SHALL NOT PASS

Woody Hayes has done as much as anyone to bring the rushing game back to football. Only in desparation will his club pass the ball more than six or seven times. So when Woody, in a fit of pique, chased Big Ten Commissioner Tug Wilson and a group of sportswriters out of Ohio State's training camp one season, Notre Dame coach Terry Brennan wryly quipped:

"You think Woody was mad that day? He was madder the next day. He caught one of his quarterbacks throwing a pass."

A DOG'S LIFE

Poor Coach McPressure passed away at the age of 42, leaving his wife very desolate. She finally bought a pup to ease her loneliness. And in time her sorrow disappeared.

"She's gotten back to her old routine," a neighbor explained. "That dog is a perfect substitute for Coach Mc-Pressure. He's out barking all day, snoozes all evening, and is fed out of cans."

CONCEIT CONCERT

The egocentric coach, arriving in Pasadena for the Rose Bowl game, went out for dinner and had to share a table with someone he didn't know. "At least," he observed, "you people out here are much more worldly wise than the people in Florida. I was once asked my name by a hotel porter! Can you imagine, he didn't know *my* name! So I told him, 'Howard Jones,' and strode out to another hotel."

"Ah ha," exclaimed the stranger, "and what *is* your real name?"

SNAP COURSE

The field house was located close to the girls' dormitory and on those warm early September practice days the boys weren't as circumspect as they should be about keeping the windows closed while dressing.

One day a note arrived from across the way: "Dear Sirs: May we suggest that you keep your windows closed or procure curtains. We do not care for a course in anatomy."

The players promptly answered: "Dear Girls: The course is entirely optional."

THE VELVET NEEDLE

Frank Howard took a lot of ribbing over the way his Clemson team was plastered by Colorado in the 1957 Orange Bowl game. Morris Frank, *Houston Chronicle* wit, put it this way:

"Frank Howard doesn't have to win at Clemson. He wisecracks his way in the winter and they forget how many he lost in the fall. But at the half of the Orange Bowl game, even Bob Hope couldn't have got him out of trouble. And before the game was over, they wished Bob Hope was coaching."

Peahead Walker, Canadian pro coach, put in the needle this way: "I asked Frank about that short kick-off play. Did he send it in? He replied, 'You don't think my boys are dumb enough to use that play on their own, do you?'"

DIGGING IN

At the Atlanta Touchdown Club's annual soiree, Wally Butts scored a quick touchdown in referring to Bobby Dodd's designation as "King of the Bowls." He drawled, "I'm not qualified to talk here with the king, but I hope to be able to crown him."

Then, answering a dig from Peahead Walker, then coach of the Canadian pro Montreal Alouettes: "I went up there to watch his team play and you should see the way they throw the ball around. Around here coaches preach control ball, but not there. One of Peahead's passers threw the kind of knuckle balls we throw here at Georgia and Peahead yelled out: 'Don't throw like that; it looks like the last show out of a Roman candle!'"

MAN OF 1,000 FACES

The wife of one of the defensive tackles on the Detroit

Lions admitted: "It's really exciting to be married to a professional tackle. Every time he comes home he looks like a different person."

STUDY IN BROWN

Rocco Pirro, assistant coach at Syracuse, will never forget the 1956 season. The Orangemen went to the Cotton Bowl and Jimmy Brown was a unanimous All-American. When the squad shoved off for their Bowl engagement, Rocco's little 8-year-old daughter broke into tears.

"Don't cry, honey," Rocco soothed. "I'll take you to the Sugar Bowl with us next year."

"You won't be going anywhere next year, Daddy," sobbed the child. "You won't have Jimmy Brown."

TALE WITH A KICK IN IT

Woody Hayes received a phone call from an alumnus in St. Louis. "Coach," he enthused, "there's a kid in the neighborhood who's the greatest athlete you ever saw."

"How much football experience has he had?" asked Woody.

"Oh, he's never played football. He's a soccer star."

"And how is a soccer player gonna help me?" inquired the Buckeye mentor.

"Use your head, Coach!" snapped the alumnus. "Imagine having a guy who can kick off with either foot?"

BOY, OH BOY!

Frank Broyles, Arkansas' head man, has four children—all boys. When the fourth was born, his boss at the time, Bobby Dodd, remarked, "Frank takes his football seriously. He's raising his own backfield."

When the bon mot was relayed to Mrs. Broyles at the hospital, she sighed, "Thank heaven, Frank's not a line coach."

THE EARLY BIRD

Frank Leahy was a stern disciplinarian who always punished tardy players with 10 laps around the track. When Johnny Lujack was married in Davenport, Leahy arrived late and apologized profusely.

"That's all right, Coach," said usher Creighton Miller, one of Leahy's former All-Americans, "just do 10 laps around the church so you won't forget to be early next time.

TIME FOR DECISION

To ease the way of their tremendous fullback, Joe Dimwit, the coaching staff manufactured an innocuous job for him in the campus kitchen. It was sorting potatoes—putting the little ones in one basket and the big ones in another.

Several hours after Dimwit went to work, the Coach dropped in to see how he was faring. He found Dimwit sitting hopelessly before the potatoes, with a very small potato in one basket and a very large one in the other. In his hand was a medium-sized potato.

"Coach," he sobbed, "I'm quitting. These decisions are killing me."

SOME NERVE!

When Frank Wiechec, trainer for the Philadelphia Phillies, worked at Temple University, he always kept a big bottle of a white liquid on top of the medicine chest. One day he walked into the training room and saw the football coach take a deep guzzle at the bottle.

"This is great stuff, Frank," said the coach. "It sure soothes my nerves."

"That's fine," replied Wiechec. "*I* use it to clean my shoes."

COIN OF THE REALM

The three football scholarship men found time lying heavily on their hands. "What'll we do tonight?" asked one.

There followed some heavy cerebration. Finally, the All-American tackle said, "I've got an idea. Let's toss a coin. If it's heads, we'll crash the fresh-soph dance. If it's tails, we'll go to the movies. And if it stands on edge, we'll study."

FAREWELL TO ARMS

Tremendous leg drive provides most of Bob White's great propulsion. At Ohio State, they tell a story about White's 17-inch-plus calf muscles. A young admirer, gaping in the locker room, remarked: "Golly, I can't even get both hands around his leg!"

One of White's teammates grinned. "Don't worry, sonny. A lot of guys *twice* your size can't even get both *arms* around it!"

CEREBRAL HEMORRHAGE

Like Bob White, the Ohio State quarterback, Frank Kremblas was a straight A student. In high school in Akron, he was seventh academically in a class of 210.

"The six students ahead of him," says Coach Woody Hayes drily, "weren't available for football. They were girls."

THE HELL OF IT

A baseball player arrived at the pearly gates where St. Peter asked him who he was. When told he was a ball player, St. Peter said, "Go to the Devil."

Some time later a basketball player arrived and upon explaining his livelihood was told to go to Hades.

The next fellow arrived at the Pearly Gates with a helmet under his arm. When asked who he was, he replied: "I'm just a poor little middle guard."

"Come on in, son," roared St. Peter. "You've been through Hell already!"

JUSTIFIABLE HOMICIDE

Watching the 1958 Pro Football All-Star Game on TV, Frank Hinek Jr., Marquette University equipment manager, heard the announcer introduce Bill George of the Bears to the viewing audience.

Hinek turned to his wife and remarked, "That's the guy who killed the Green Bay Packers last season."

The voice of seven-year-old Bronk Hinek quickly interpolated: "Daddy, did he get jail for that?"

READING MATTER

The famous actress, Arlene Francis, has a 12-year-old son, Peter. One day he was assigned to do a book report and decided to undertake *The Hunchback of Notre Dame*.

"That's pretty tough going," his mother warned him.

"Well, that's what I'd like to read," he said. So she bought him the book.

A few days later he screamed, "Mama, that book is 491 pages long and there's not a word in it about George Izo!"

GOLDEN RULE

The Rockne-Zuppke "feud" was one of the wittiest in history. At a banquet after the 1924 season, Zuppke concluded his speech as follows: "Well, Rock, you and your Four Horsemen had a lot of luck this year. I suppose instead of giving them gold footballs you'll give them gold horseshoes."

Rockne promptly rose to his feet and retorted: "Your suggestion about giving the gold horseshoes is a good one, Zupp. But after looking over your defeats this season, I suggest that instead of golden balls, you give your team golden skids."

STROKE OF FORTUNE

The two small-time football coaches were shooting the breeze, "Wouldn't it be great," said one, "if you beat Notre Dame, Oklahoma, Michigan State, Maryland, and Georgia Tech all in one season, then went on to the Rose Bowl and trounced UCLA. What would you do if that happened?"

The other coach pondered a moment. "Well," he finally said, "I'd send my assistant coach to California to collect all the trophies and make the big speech to the press."

"You mean you wouldn't bother going yourself?" asked the other incredulously.

"How could I?" replied the other. "I'd already be dead from the shock!"

WILLY-NILLY BILLY

When Billy Vessels joined the Baltimore Colts, he was a David in a camp full of Goliaths. The little fellow had to look up at such monsters as 270-lb. Art Donovan, 275-lb.

Tom Finnin, 255-lb. Don Joyce, 245-lb. Gino Marchetti, 305-lb. Buzz Clark, 270-lb. Don Chelf, etc.

Nobody seemed to pay any attention to him, and he began figuring that he had done something wrong and that the players were deliberately snubbing him. So he went over to publicist John Steadman and told him of his troubles.

Kindly John patted him on the shoulder. "Relax, Billy," he advised. "They're not cold-shouldering you. They just haven't seen you yet!"

THE HEISMAN COMETH

A Shakespearean actor in his spare time, "Old John" Heisman had a predilection for the rich, round phrase. On the first day of practice every year, he'd display a football to his squad and ask, "What is it?", then proceed to answer his own question:

"A prolate spheroid—that is, an elongated sphere—in which the outer leathern casing is drawn tightly over a somewhat smaller rubber tubing." Then he would add ominously:

"Better to have died as a small boy than to fumble this."

SHORT-SIGHTED

Heisman's 1912 Georgia Tech team featured a 155-pound center named Al Loeb. Heisman was fond of calling him a physical misfortune and once asked him how he managed to stand up to all the big men he faced.

"Coach," cracked Loeb, "I'm nearsighted and can't see how big they are."

IN DRYDOCK

The selfsame Al Loeb once helped coach the Federal

Penitentiary eleven. During one game, played in a downpour, a prisoner insisted that Loeb borrow his denim jacket.

Though his only suit was being drenched, Loeb demurred. He thought it unmanly of a coach—until another prisoner chimed in: "Go ahead and take his jacket, coach. He's got 20 years to dry off in."

GRUNT IN AID

The head coach was a grumpy, taciturn old bugger, and the sophomore halfback complained to the assistant coach. "You can't get a nice word out of him. No matter what you do, he just gives you an 'ugh' or an 'agh.'"

"He's not such a bad guy," soothed the assistant coach. "It's just that you have to take a lot for grunted."

QUICK, WATSON

If you're looking for a barrel of chuckles, don't miss Emmett Watson's article, "Don't Raise Your Boy to Be a Football Coach," in *Sport*. Sherlock Holmes would have loved the guy. He'd never have had to hiss, "Quick Watson, the needle!" The Watson who authorized this piece is a needler of monstrous proportions. Witness these needle-pointed gems:

"Don't raise your boy to be a football coach. In fact, be more cautious than that. At the first sign of his desire to become a football coach, just stop raising him."

"Football coaches are a class of selfless sufferers who go on building character year after year, no matter how many states they have to import it from."

"Where else but in football can you be sure of that exhilarating day-to-day experience of wondering whether you have a job?"

"My figures on athletic directors show that they usually fire two coaches and then leave with the third. This athletic director (I know)is working on his second coach."

"Just before the game, the whole squad got food poisoning. They had to keep dashing on and off the field, back and forth. They were compelled by a force stronger than the coach's will."

AILIN' PHELAN

Jimmy Phelan coached at Missouri, Purdue, Washington, and St. Mary's before going to the pros. His troubles didn't exactly end there, either. Three franchises—the Los Angeles Dons, the N. Y. Yanks, and the Dallas Texans—went down under him.

"When I was with the Yanks," Phelan once said, "a report got around that there was some kind of animal loose in Yankee Stadium. The groundkeeper said he thought it was a fox. But when they caught it, it wasn't a fox at all. Just one of those wolves that followed me all the way from Seattle."

GRACE-FUL GESTURE

A famous football coach tells this one about his first coaching job at a tough little mid-Atlantic college. It was dinner time and he walked into the dorm where the training table was set up. Noticing all the players sitting around the table, he pulled up a chair and said, "Well, let's eat."

Nobody made a move. So the coach repeated, "Come on, fellers, let's dig in."

Another silence. Finally a beetle-browed monster cleared his throat and explained, "Hell, coach, we ain't prayed yet."

HAIR-RAISER

The coach was applying for a raise. "I've been with you 25 years," he told the athletic board, "and I've never asked you for a raise before."

"That," retorted the chairman of the board, "is why you've been coaching here for 25 years."

MASHED POTATOES

Monstrous 265-lb. Earl Leggett is about as easy to move as Boulder Dam and when he lowers the boom on you, it's good night, sweetheart. Against Arkansas one year, he was downright murderous. In one sequence of plays, he flattened the ball-carrier three straight times.

On the next play, Arkansas tried the opposite guard, Paul Ziegler. Paul grabbed the ball-carrier by one leg, but couldn't bring him down. After several seconds of tugging, the LSU guard looked up at the runner and begged:

"For gosh sakes fall down before Leggett gets in here and mashes both of us!"

A COUPLE OF GROUPS

The ex-California mastermind, Pappy Waldorf, is a large gent who weighs in the vicinity of 275 pounds. One day he addressed his squad as follows: "You're not only a fine football team, you're a fine group as well."

Touched by this tribute, one of the players, Jim Cullom, replied, "And you're a fine group yourself, Coach."

SHORT WAY HOME

Trying to book a game with a Pennsylvania school, the Texas coach put in a long distance call and was told that the toll would be $2.

"Why," the Texan sputtered, "back home we can talk to hell and back for two bucks."

"Mebbe so," answered the operator, "but from Texas that's a local call."

STERN TASKMASTER

"Portrait by Bill Stern" authorized by Vic Gold in *The Skiff* (Texas Christian U.):

One fall day in South Bend, Ind., a small, anemic-looking lad approached Coach Frank Leahy. "Coach," the kid said, "I wanna play football for Notre Dame."

"G'wan punk," the coach said. "You'd be broken in two."

But the gritty young kid insisted. Day after day he reported to the field and registered his desire to play football for Notre Dame. Finally, out of sheer anger, Coach Leahy agreed. "Report to the dressing room right before game time Saturday. I'll give you a uniform."

That Saturday, the boy showed up promptly. Leahy was surprised to see the young, spindle-legged kid. The genial coach smiled.

"Well," he said, putting his hand on the boy's shoulder, "if you hink you're going to play for one of my teams and screw up the works, you're nuts."

The freshman was crushed. But the coach, ever mindful of a youngster's feelings, tried to soften the blow.

"You're just not built for football, kid. Why don't you go to China and get into politics instead?"

That young boy—turned down by the Notre Dame coach —followed that advice.

His name: Chiang Kai-shek.

WHICH WAY TO THE GOAL?

One of the least stodgy coaches in the football lodge, Duffy Daugherty is still operating on the football-can-be-fun theory. Rehearsing a new pass pattern, he told his charges, "This play will go all the way." Whereupon Pat Wilson threw the ball—only to see it intercepted and returned for a touchdown by the scrubs.

Chuckles broke out among the Spartan squad. But Duffy remained unfazed.

"You'll notice," he said, "that I didn't say which way."

COMPLIMENTARY CRACK

When it came to complimentary tickets, Knute Rockne was a tough nut to crack. It took ingenuity to disgorge any Annie Oakleys out of him. One afternoon Joe Savoldi, the great fullback, braced him for a couple of ducats.

"How about two for Saturday," Savoldi asked, a twinkle in his eye.

"Relatives?" Rockne asked.

"No, tickets," Savoldi replied.

THE MATERIALIST

Clair Bee, the fabulous ex-college and pro hoop coach who's now athletic-directing the N. Y. Military Academy, devastated the 200 coaches and officials attending a recent Westchester County (N.Y.) Sports Forum.

His is the kind of natural wit that pours out in a wonderfully funny stream: "You know, I came to New York as a football coach. Now, we didn't have any material to speak of. So I took a trip to the mine country in West Virginia. I couldn't have arrived at the mines at a better time. Lewis had called a strike—and I was able to return to New York with a flock of fine students."

QUIZ KID

In one of those early-season written quiz reviews, the football coach loaded his squad down with enough problems to keep them engaged for at least 90 minutes. He then leaned back in his chair for a little rest.

Ten minutes later he was startled to see his big dumb tackle rise and ask: "Do you have any more of these problems, Coach?"

"You mean you've finished all those I assigned?" the mentor asked incredulously.

"Oh, no," replied the tackle, "I couldn't answer any of these, so I thought I might have better luck with some others!"

HANDY MAN

Frank Gifford, the N. Y. Giants' halfback, is one of those versatile fellows who can do just about everything superlatively well. He's a tremendous runner, passer, kicker, and defensive ace. In 1959, he insisted on trying his hand as a T qb, then on place kicking. To prove he wasn't kidding around, he kicked three field goals against the Bears in an exhibition game.

"Gifford does so many things so well," commented Captain Kyle Rote, "that he's put more men out of work than Eli Whitney."

ZOO SAID IT!

Rather than see his kiddies go hungry, the unemployed

football coach accepted an offer from the local zoo to wear a gorilla skin and entertain the tots on week-ends. The first Sunday he was doing all right swinging on a bar, until a chain snapped and catapulted him into the next cage— occupied by a huge lion. The king of beasts stared at him balefully and the coach started screaming for help.

Then a whisper reached him: "For cripes sake, buddy, shut up. You're not the only coach out of work!"

TRUCKIN' ON DOWN

Roosevelt Grier plays such a tremendous defensive right tackle for the pro Giants that his teammates call him "Truck"; everybody is afraid to pass him on the right!

BOYS WILL BE BOYS

Though Boys H. S. in New York City had four kids named Williams on the football squad of 33, Coach Wally Muller remained unperturbed and unconfused.

"I have a formula," he declared. "Whenever I praised one of them, I used his first name. When a bawling-out was in order, I just referred to Williams. That kept all of 'em on their toes!"

DOPE ON DUFFY

At Michigan State, Duffy Daugherty is firmly ensconced as a mastermind and a wit par excellence. One day he received a letter addressed to "Duffy the Dope."

"Didn't that make you mad?" he was asked.

"I didn't mind getting the card," he replied. "It was pretty funny. The thing that bothered me was that the East Lansing post office knew exactly where to deliver it."

SPELLING BEE

The Gunnery, an exclusive prep school in Connecticut, was being beaten 35-13, by its arch rival, Canterbury, and the time had come for the school's "long yell."

"Give me a G!" exhorted the Gunnery cheerleader, and the students roared in heartening response. The aim, of course, was to roar through all the letters in Gunnery. But the cheerleader, having got his G, threw everyone into confusion by next demanding: "Give me an E!"

The startled cheering section gave him nothing much (reports *Sports Illustrated*). But an English teacher responded in a loud clear voice:

"In spelling, I give you F."

IT TAKES THE BLIND

The near-sighted trainer had broken his glasses that morning and wasn't rightly prepared for the visit of the big injured tackle. Hoping to bluff his way through, he boomed, "Glad to see you, boy! What's bothering you today?"

"My ribs, doc. I missed my assignment on No. 27 and they really unloaded on me."

"Well, take your clothes off, son, and let me have a look at it."

The trainer then started poking a finger here and there. Finally, he sighed, "Those ribs, sticking out that way. I don't like it."

"Doc," moaned the athlete, "if it's all the same to you, pay some attention to me—and stop fiddling with that venetian blind."

COURSE OF ACTION

It was a freshman English course and a brawny football

player kept interrupting the prof. The exasperated prof finally blew his stack. "Look here, mister," he snapped, "I've been teaching this course for years, and I think I know a little more about it than you do."

"I'm sorry, sir," retorted the athlete, "but this is the third time I've taken it, and I think I know something about it, too!"

DEFENSIVE PURSUIT

The guy was a pro end with a very shady reputation as a dirty player. One of his fouls cost the club the league title and at the All-Star game in January his coach bitterly asked: "Have you made any New Year's resolutions yet?"

"Yup," replied the rowdy, "from now on I'm going to follow the Ten Commandments."

"You've been following them all your life," snapped the coach. "Why don't you resolve to catch up with them this year?"

MISTAKEN IDENTITY

Larry Killick and another fugitive from the North watched the TCU-Syracuse Bowl game from deep in the heart of the Texas Christian rooting section. Larry's buddy, a hardy soul, let his enthusiasm get away from him as Syracuse stormed up from behind.

As the TCU delegation watched in glum silence, Syracuse staged a stirring drive. Larry's buddy rose to his feet and, much to Larry's horror, started roaring: "C'mon Syracuse, chaw them Rebels up! Get 'em Syracuse! C'mon you Yankees!"

Larry grabbed his pal by the coattails. "For God's sake," he pleaded, "sit down before you get killed! Who do you think you are?"

His buddy thought for a moment, then his face brightened:

"Custer!" he roared.

A SPIT IN TIME

It was one of those pro-championship games played in Chicago in late December with the icy blasts ripping in from Lake Michigan. As the Bears lined up to start the second half, the referee noticed that only eight men were on the field.

"Where are the tackles and the center?" he yelled to the quarterback.

"They're getting patched up by the trainer," snapped the qb. "They got knocked down by flying ice."

"Flying ice?" echoed the ref.

"You heard me," replied the qb. "They tried to spit against the wind!"

A BLOCKER'S LAMENT

The man who blocks for the backs
Must deprive himself every dream
Of glory in headlines and lacks
Any chance to star for the team.

The man who blocks for the backs
Must take a bad beating and grin,
Pile opponents in untidy stacks,
And when able, not lead with his chin.

The man who blocks for the backs
Gets bruised and beaten and wrenched,
If a back becomes careless or lax—
It's the blocker who's usually benched.

The man who blocks for the backs
When penalized, his life becomes grim—
The ref stops the play and then acts,
And the coach "blows the whistle" on him.

The man who blocks for the backs
Must be leopard, and horse, or a mule,
And if under the pressure he cracks,
He's a "jar-headed" goof or a fool.

The men that block for the backs
In losing, will shoulder the blame,
In vict'ry, however, these facts
Are obscured, and the backs win the fame.

Yes, the men who block for the backs
Are said to be plumb off their rockers,
But dumber by far are the sacks
Who get blocked by the other team's blockers.

—By JOSEPH MAMANA
Principal, Governor Wolf Jr. H. S.
Easton, Penna.

16 GAMES (*With Apologies to Tennessee Ernie*)

Some people say a coach is made out of steel,
A mind that is blank and a heart that can't feel;
All muscle and bone and a boasting way,
No ability to play but to holler all day.

Played 16 games and what do I get?
Another season older and not a win yet.
St. Peter, don't call me, 'cause I can't go,
I owe the officials all of my dough.

The Alumni say that I have material to spare;
I've got a four-foot center when he stands on a chair,
There's a 90-pound tackle and an 80-pound guard,
They should be all muscle but they're 100% lard.

Played 16 matches and what do I get?
Another season older and not a win yet.
St. Peter, don't call me to the celestial shore,
I've lost 16 games but we're going to play more.

The season starts way early in the fall,
Working from sun up to dark, throwing out the ball,
Get home dead tired and ready for bed,
But have to make lesson plans to earn my bread.

Played 16 games and what do I get?
Another season older and not a win yet.
St. Peter, please call me—I must leave here,
They burned me in effigy again this year!

> By Ross J. WILLINK
> *Maryvale H. S.*
> *Cheektowaga, N. Y.*

LIKE FATHER, LIKE SON

Duffy Daugherty's little son came home one day after trying out for a midget football team. Duffy, evincing a fatherly interest, asked what position he was playing.

"I'm not playing any position," replied the youngster.

"Why not?" asked Duffy in surprise.

"Because," replied the youngster, "they found out I couldn't block or tackle or run or pass. All I could do was yell. So they made me coach."

BACK ROAD TO SUCCESS

After observing his first rowing race, the football coach remarked: "That's for me. It's the only sport I ever saw where you could sit on your fanny and win going backward."

JIMINY CRIMMINS

In his last year at Indiana, Bernie Crimmins was approached by a sympathetic alumnus who asked: "Coach, are we being out-offensed or out-defensed?"

"Neither," snapped Bernie. "Out-recruited."

LOW FINANCE

The high school principal warned the recently hired football coach not to reveal the financial terms of his contract.

"You can count on me," replied the coach. "I'm just as ashamed of it as you are."

SUCCESSOR STORY

Tired of being the conference doormat, the college president decided to lend a hand in the recruiting. He toured a number of school gridirons and then returned and called in his coach.

"How did you make out?" asked the mentor.

"Well, I saw one team that went through a 12-game schedule unbeaten, untied and unscored-on. The amazing thing about it was that their line averaged just 145 pounds, their backfield 135, and they had no passer or kicker."

"Well," said the coach. "You didn't waste any scholarships on them."

"No," replied the president, "but I hired their coach as your successor."

DAILY SCRUBBING

During the summer hiatus, the first-string Iowa State guard met one of the Oklahoma scrubs.

"I suppose you're looking forward to the season," said the Oklahoma player.

"I sure am," replied the Iowa State tackle. "But I certainly hate to think about our game with your team."

"What are you kicking about?" answered the Oklahoma scrub. "You only meet 'em once during the season. We play 'em every few days."

UNREQUIRED READING

The coach of a little college wrote to Forest Evashevski, explaining that he had always been a Straight T advocate but had introduced the Winged T to his frosh team the past season, and now the freshmen were beating the varsity regularly. Where, he asked in concluding the letter, could he get a copy of Evashevski's book, *Scoring Power with the Winged T Offense.*

"Dear Coach," replied Evashevski. "Congratulations on installing the Winged T. But as I see it, it should be three years before you have need for my book."

BELL RINGER

"What would happen," Bert Bell, pro football czar, was asked at a luncheon, "if a team was trying to kick the extra point and the ball burst in the air with half going over the bar and half under it?"

"The way I see it," remarked Bell after cogitating a moment, "the team would be out about 18 bucks."

BY YOUR LEAVE

The star tackle stormed into the coach's office and raged, "If the dean doesn't take back what he said to me, I'm going to leave college."

"What did he say?" asked the amazed coach.

"He told me to leave college."

A DOG'S LIFE

The coach was a caustic, sarcastic buck who chewed out his squad from morn till night, five days a week and all afternoon on Saturday. At the end of the season, the squad was amazed when the captain passed the hat around for donations to buy the coach a present.

But they all chipped in when they saw the gift: A handsomely framed portrait of Lassie inscribed: "With love, from Mother."

THE WRONG PLAY

At a classroom skull session, the coach laid out his plays on the desk, then left the room for a moment. While he was out, one of the ends placed a basketball play among the diagrams.

When the coach returned, he went over the plays one by one, saying, "This is a fullback counter, this is an end sweep, this is an end around, etc."

Eventually he came to the basketball play. "And this," he said, holding it up, "is a piece of confounded impudence."

BRAY OF SUNSHINE

The sports columnist who had attacked the local football coach in his paper was embarrassed when he met the coach at a downtown quarterback's luncheon the next afternoon.

"I'm genuinely sorry I wrote that column," the writer apologized. "I guess I'm just a jackass."

"Don't say that," replied the coach. "You're no more of a jackass than I am."

"That," murmured the columnist, unable to restrain himself, "is close enough."

MAKING PILES

When Frank Leahy was a tackle at Notre Dame, the varsity was running plays at the scrubs. Three straight times the famous Irish off-tackle play was stopped at the line of scrimmage. Each time the offensive tackle (Leahy) and the ball-carried wound up at the bottom of the pile.

After the third time, Knute Rockne walked over to Leahy. "Frank," he said, "I always knew you were a great defensive tackle, but I didn't know how great until you piled up three of our plays while playing offense."

IN THE BAG

The former Missouri coach, Don Faurot, claims that a football coach who's forced to resign under pressure is very much like the mischievous little son of a young widowed mother who was so bad he was the talk of the town.

Eventually his mother remarried and several months later the boy was asked how he was getting along with his new father.

"Fine," said the boy. "He takes me out hunting in the woods and lets me walk back all by myself. He takes me fishing out in the middle of the big lake and lets me swim back to shore."

"Don't you find swimming all that distance quite a feat?" asked the shocked townfolk.

"Not at all," replied the boy. "There's nothing to it once I get out of the sack."

HOARSE AND BUGGY

The football coach was checking in his team at a small hotel when he noticed a black spot on the register. "What's this?" he asked.

"Only a bug, sir," replied the clerk.

The coach flung down the pen. "I don't mind bugs in a hotel, but when the damned alumni crawl out of the woodwork to see what room I'm assigned—that's too much."

THE BATTLE OF LEXICON

By DAN PARKER, *Sports Editor, N. Y. Daily Mirror*
(Reprinted by special permission)

Quarterback—a refund from the 25¢ gas meter in the dressing room.

Split T—when the Oolang bag breaks in the boiling water.

Tail Back—what a decaudated bulldog never gets, once the vet chops it off.

Flat Zone—where the building ordinances permit tenement houses.

Cross Buck—an irritated elk.

Coffin Corner—where the caskets are kept handy to smuggle the dead off the field.

Offensive Back—a bad case of lumbago.

Sidelines—what all the players have in college.

Charging—what boys in the Pacific Coast Conference were doing for their services.

Placement Kick—a boot delivered where a guy needs it most.

Cut-Off Block—what the English did to Mary Queen of Scots.

Hand-Off—a command often heard in the stands at co-ed institutions.

Man in Motion—that Elvis Presley guy.

Single Wing Left—the remains of a Thanksgiving turkey.

Check-Off—a great Russian short story writer.

Hook Passes—to steal punched tickets for game.

Reversing the Field—turning the gridiron sod upside down when it's worn out on one side.

Touchback—when you ask a guy to lend you that ten-spot you let him have a year ago.

Inside-Out Block—a repair job on your autumn fedora.

Cut-Backs—reductions in players' salaries during periodic economy waves.

Banana Pass—one which calls for the split.

End Around—the approximate time the game will be over.

Grant in Aid—when Ulysses S. helped capture Richmond.

Uprights—colleges that claim to be purer because their payoff checks don't bounce.

Flood Pass—a card which permits you to walk right in over your head.

Fullback Swing—a porch hammock you can't fall over backwards out of.

Tackles Back—two linemen returning to alma mater after a sabbatical year in pro football.

Safety—something you'll find in numbers if you talk out of turn.

Right Tackle—the proper rod for catching a certain type of fish.

Fair Catch—the other fellow's date at a post-game party.

Linebacker—a fellow who's ready to make good his boasts.

Pivots—teeth to replace those knocked out during the game.

Reverses—what the best of teams run into.

Unbalanced Line—the chatter of a guy who's slightly off the beam.

Pass Protection—what the team press agent needs on day of big game.

In and Out Run—office maneuver executed by experts on days when they want to get in an afternoon of golf.

Blocking Angle—a girder that cuts off our view from the stands.

SHAKESPEARE ON FOOTBALL

By Lou Darvas *in The Sporting News*

My dull brain was wrought with things forgotten."
Macbeth, Act 1 Scene 3

"But now, I am cabined, cribbed, confined, bound in."
Macbeth, Act 3 Scene 2

"You blocks, you stones, you worse than senseless things!"
Julius Caesar, Act 1 Scene 1

"I can see yet without spectacles and I see no such matter."
Much Ado about Nothing, Act 1 Scene 1

"What, ho! What, ho!—A messenger from the galleys."
Othello, Act 1 Scene 3

"O poor Orlando, thou art overthrown."
As you like it, Act 1 Scene 2

II

HOOPING IT UP

SHOOTING STYLE

When Bob Mlkvy played his first varsity game for Penn, in the stands proudly rooting for him was his famous All-American brother of Temple fame, Bill.

At the half, a newsman remarked to Bill: "The kid shoots just like you did—all the time."

PERIPATETIC PRESS

Defensing Wilt Chamberlain has become the prime coaching headache of the NBA. Big Ed Macauley, the witty Hawks' mentor, has come up with the only sensible solution. "Next time out we're going to triple-team him, and if that doesn't work we're going to start pressing him in the locker room."

SMOKE SCREAM

Sure sign of collegiate basketball's comeback at Madison Square Garden is the jocular signs being held aloft by the student rooters. When St. Joseph's of Philadelphia visited town, the St. John's boosters unfurled a poster reading: "Philly isn't a city; it's a cigar."

PERPETUAL LOSER

After losing their fifth straight game, the Knicks boarded a plane from Syracuse. Wing-ice delayed the flight for hours, and a raging storm was battled all the way to LaGuardia. Coming down the runway, Coach Carl Braun, who had bought the limit of flight insurance at the Syracuse airport, threw up his hands disgustedly and said, "Lost another!"

LOGGERSHEAD REVISITED

The battle of words among Ken Loeffler, the officials, and
Everett Case after North Carolina State nosed out La Salle,
76-74, at Raleigh, N. C., back in 1951, made newspaper
headlines for days. Then the controversy apparently died.

The following summer Loeffler and Case were flying
across the Atlantic for a clinic in Germany, when the pilot
announced that the plane would be unable to land at Keflavik, Iceland, and would have to proceed to Scotland. Case,
sleeping, was jolted awake by Loeffler.

"Everett," roared the fierce LaSalle coach, "we can't land
at Keflavik. We're going on to Scotland and may not make
it. Quick, before we go down, *admit those officials at Raleigh
were terrible!*"

FOR WHOM THE BELLS TOLL

Of his coaching career in the professional ranks, Ken
Loeffler says it was like crowding 15 years of coaching into
three years.

"I've been asked why I left the pros," he declares. "Well,
there were two contributing factors. One was the terrific
toll the pro game takes on your health, and the other was
George Mikan."

ROUSING RECEPTION

Having won the Texas State hoop crown for the first time
in the history of the school, the coach returned to a rousing
reception. At the huge banquet that evening, he was lion-
ized to a fare-thee-well. Finally, he got to his feet: "Ladies
and gentlemen," he started. At which point a big, happy,
red-faced Texan leaped up and bellowed:

"Thatta boy, Coach, you're a-talkin' right down my
alley!"

WORK PROGRAM

With some coaches' salaries being what they are, we got a chuckle out of the following *bon mot*: The way for a coach to earn a good annual salary is to work two years.

STAND-UP GUY

Early in the season, Bob Pettit had one of his worst games in New York, scoring just 11 points. Next time he hit the big city one of the local scribes asked him whether he was thinking of atoning for his previous game.

"I don't know what you're talking about," said Bob with a straight face. "Right after that game I went to my psychiatrist and he convinced me that it never happened."

"Go on," replied the scribe, getting into the spirit of it. "You couldn't possibly go to a psychiatrist. No one has a couch big enough for you."

"Who said anything about a couch?" snapped the big fellow right back. "My psychiatrist stands me in a closet during treatments."

SPANISH BEDLAM

"For sheer bedlam," claims the international coach, Jim McGregor, "it's impossible to beat basketball in Spain. They get so excited you can't even hear the ref's whistle. A whistle blows but nothing stops. The teams go right on playing until there's a slight lull. Then the referee comes over and says, 'The last six baskets didn't count.'"

MEATY BONES

Bones McKinney, Wake Forest coach, is fracturing the hoop beat with such "lay-ups" as:

"I know a basketball coach who had a lifetime contract.

He had one bad season and what do you suppose happened to him? The college president called him in, pronounced him dead, and then fired him in the same breath."

"We're just a bunch of southerners—country boys—mostly from the southern end of Pennsylvania."

"I'm glad basketball could foster a sport like football. You know, a football is just an old basketball that has lost its shape."

DIZZY HEIGHTS

Late last summer Power Memorial High (New York City) basketball coach Jack Donahue received an unexpected phone call from Junius Kellogg, former Manhattan College basketball star.

"Jack," said Junie, "my kid brother just came to New York from Virginia to live with me. He's 16, he'll be a junior, and plays a little basketball. He's a pretty good student and, oh yes, Jack, he's seven feet tall.

"Jack . . . Jack . . . Jack, why don't you answer me?"

UNEMBARRASSING MOMENT

Ohio State's crack frosh five had just finished beating the varsity for the second time last winter when a reporter approached Coach Fred Taylor and asked if it wasn't embarrassing to see his varsity beaten by the freshmen.

"I'll tell you," said Taylor after a pause. "I'd feel a lot worse if they were someone else's freshmen!"

TO FORGIVE IS DIVINE

"You won't catch me getting ulcers," boasted the new head coach. "For one thing I take things as they come. And for another, although I often get angry, I don't hold a grudge—

not even against referees who've done things to me I'll *never* forgive."

SUB PAR

With 10 seconds to play and the score 85-32, the losing coach sent a sub sprinting into the game.

"Now what can a sub do in that situation?" remarked a sportswriter.

"He's probably bringing in a play," grunted a fellow scribe.

BLUES IN THE NIGHT

The basketball coach was moaning about his star player to the publicity man. "As a soph he was the nation's No. 6 scorer. As a junior he topped the country with a 38-point average. And in our first four games he averaged 40 points a game."

"So what are you crying about?" asked the amazed publicist.

"I ask you," retorted the coach, "what has he done for me lately?"

CHEERFUL EARFUL

The veteran coach was counseling his youthful replacement. "You'll discover that in nearly every skull session some youngster will be eager to argue. Your first impulse will be to silence him. I advise you to think carefully before doing so. He'll probably be the only one listening."

THANKS FOR THE MEMORY

"How can we ever show our appreciation?" gushed the

superintendent to the coach at the banquet commemorating
an all-victorious season.

"Sir," replied the coach drily, "ever since the Phoenicians
invented money, there's been only one answer to that question."

FENCING IN OSCAR

Bones McKinney, colorful Wake Forest basketball coach,
was puzzling over a defense against the great Oscar Robertson when one of his players piped up, "Coach, why don't
you use the box-and-one?"

"What's that?" asked Bones.

"Why, put four men on Robertson and one on the rest
of the team."

FOOD FOR THOUGHT

The pro basketball coach was notorious for "chewing out"
players who made mistakes. One evening he inserted a
rookie in a key situation, who promptly lost the ball on a
wild pass, costing the ball game.

As the youngster fearfully approached the bench, ready
to be eaten alive, he saw his coach on his knees, apparently
praying. The lad kneeled beside the coach and said, "Coach,
I'm delighted to join you in prayer when only a moment
ago I feared for my life."

"Shut up!" snapped the coach. "I'm saying grace."

ALL-SEEING EYE

In the 1958 Carousel Tournament, Bill Reinhart, George
Washington hoop coach, complained to an official about one
of his calls. "And don't tell me I couldn't see the play from
where I was sitting," Reinhart warned. "I've been officiating
from that place for 40 years."

TRUSS-FUL NATURE

The basketball coach was exhorting one of his normally fine defensive players to greater effort. "You can't let your man run around loose," he snapped. "your teammates are working hard to get a few points. They need your support."

"Gosh, Coach," replied the boy, "it's home. I forgot it when I packed my gear this afternoon."

MORTAL SILENCE

Upon returning to the coaching room after absenting himself from a skull session, the basketball coach was astonished to discover all his players sitting in deathly silence. Since this was highly unusual, he asked for an explanation.

The team's playmaker spoke up boldly: "Well, you once told us that if you ever left the room and came back to find everyone sitting perfectly still, you'd drop dead."

WHAT'S NUDE?

The little backcourt playmaker, attempting to cut down the middle, heard something snap. Before he could reach down, his pants suddenly dropped to his ankles. And there he stood in the middle of the floor, *trés dishabille.*

"Poor guy," murmured one of the boys in the press box, "he reminds me of a newly born baby."

"How come?" asked a nearby reporter.

"He's small, he's red, and he needs help."

TACITURN OF THE SCREW

The head coach and his assistant were a taciturn pair who hated to make speeches. At a dinner one evening, they were scheduled to speak—unbeknownst to either. The toastmaster called on Coach Hoxie.

"There must be some mistake," stammered Hoxie. "Coach Byrnes is the one who does the talking."

The toastmaster turned to Byrne. The latter stood up and said, "Hoxie just made the speech."

TRAVELOGUE

To kick off the 1958-59 basketball season, the pro Detroit Pistons conducted one of those complete-this-sentence-in-25-words-or-less contests, on "I like the Detroit Pistons because . . ."

The most amusing entry was turned in by Kit Smith, 11-year-old son of the Pistons publicity man. His entry read: "I like the Detroit Pistons because I do not live in St. Louis, Minneapolis, Cincinnati, New York, Boston, Philadelphia, or Syracuse."

AROUND SHE GOES

Basketball fans stopped worrying about the Russians' satellite as soon as they learned that the gadget was about the size of a basketball. As one real hoop fan puts it, "We'll have one up there as soon as the season starts, the way kids shoot nowadays."

THE RIM OF MADNESS

Pete Newell, California hoop coach, bemoaning his lack of talent: "The shooting of our team is so bad that when the janitor took the rim off the backboard to make some repairs the other day, our boys played 45 minutes before they missed it."

INDISPENSABLE COACH

The basketball coach was called for jury duty. He begged

to be excused on the grounds that he couldn't afford to be away from his team. The judge scoffed, "I suppose you're one of those people who think the world couldn't go 'round without them."

"No, your honor," replied the coach. "I know very well my team can get along without me. But I can't afford to let them find it out."

HELL-BENT FOR ELECTION

The pro hoop coach, a strict disciplinarian unhappy about his team's condition, decided to make a surprise bed-time check. He went up to his big center's room and knocked on the door. No answer. Suspecting the worst, he turned the knob and walked in.

A cloud of cigar smoke assailed his nostrils. "Cappy," he called, "are you here?" No answer. So he started tracking down the smoke. It led to the bathroom. He pushed open the door and saw a huge spiral of smoke rising from the circular shower curtain. The coach separated the curtain and there was his star player—clad in pajamas with a huge stogie in his mouth.

"Cappy," the coach sternly rasped, "what are you doing here?"

"Coach," the big boy replied coolly, flicking the ash from his cigar, "better shut that curtain. I'm voting."

DOUBLE DRIBBLE

The kids at Dolph Schayes Basketball Camp had just been given a lecture on the value of keeping the ball off the floor and not dribbling so much. In the very first scrimmage after the seminar, one of the kids promptly went dribble crazy. From the sidelines came the caustic voice of Counselor Jon Cincebox:

"Look, Zinc, if you want to dribble, go to Cousy's camp."

FOUL SHOOTING

Dolph Schayes is one of the greatest foul shooters in the world, leading the NBA in 1957-58 with a .904 average. During the summer, he took his wife to the state fair in Syracuse. One of the booths featured a foul-shooting game with some nice prizes for anyone who could sink five shots in a row. Mrs. Schayes promptly got after her hubby to win some of the prizes for her.

Dolph, an extremely modest fellow, demurred at first but had to give in when his spouse persisted. He then took up his position behind the line and began sinking one after another—while the huckster in the booth paled with dismay.

As Dolph cleaned the booth of all the better prizes, sinking 25 shots in a row, a large crowd gathered around him. Finally, a little old woman tapped Dolph on the shoulder and said:

"Look, Mister, I don't know who you are, but I'm sure my son would like your autograph."

DRESS REHEARSAL

After West Virginia snapped North Carolina's 37-game winning streak, the Tar Heel coach, Frank McGuire, went into the Mountaineer dressing room to congratulate them.

One of the sportswriters, impressed by this exhibition of graciousness, shook Frank's hand and said, "That was a mighty fine speech, sir."

"It should be," smiled McGuire. "I've been practicing it for 37 games."

SALARY CONFERENCE

Ever wonder what really goes on in a salary conference

in professional sports? Leonard Koppett, *New York Post* columnist, sat in on the confab between Ben Kerner, owner of the St. Louis Hawks, and one of his back-court men, Al Ferrari, and says it went like this.

Al, fresh out of the service, was greeted by Kerner as follows: "Now, Al, I've thought it over very carefully and analyzed it all out and I've got a certain figure in mind for you. I've taken into consideration the time you've been away, and just exactly how you fit into our plans. I know you can help us and assuming you come through, you're worth this certain sum. I'm sure you'll agree it's a fair amount.

"I don't want you to think you can make up in one lump two years of being in service, but I've calculated that in, and the figure I've got here is going to satisfy you, I think. In relation to other figures we have, you'll admit that it's a good proposition and I'm certainly not going to haggle if you don't think so, but this amount . . ."

And so on and so on for a half hour until Ferrari was ready to scream, "What's the figure?" Just as he was about to open his mouth, Kerner interrupted himself and said:

"So tell me—what do you think you should get?"

CONFIRMATION TO FOLLOW

Alan Seiden, St. John's U. great little back-court driver in 1958-59, has been a dedicated basketball player ever since he was a kid. His room was a miniature gym. He had a basket hung up and his friends used to play games in there.

One day when he was in his room with his rabbi studying for his confirmation, his parents thought it would be nice to take a candid picture of the two of them at work. So they entered the room—and found Alan shooting at the basket, with the rabbi sitting pathetically in the corner.

"What's going on?" Mr. Seiden asked in amazement.

The rabbi shrugged. "Alan told me if I didn't look at his set shot, he wouldn't study."

EMBARRASSING MOMENT

Informed that two basketball teams were aboard, the plane captain gave a cheery salutation over the p. a. system.

"We wish to welcome the University of Kentucky basketball team and congratulate it on its victory last night."

Silence. Minutes later the embarrassed captain's voice again boomed.

"I wish to apologize for the oversight, but we have another team aboard. We welcome the University of Arkansas basketball team."

In the cabin, the players from Xavier University and the University of Tulsa—the only passengers in the plane—broke into wild laughter.

IN THE BAG

In a tough, fist-swinging game for the Missouri Valley crown, Cincinnati overcame a 10-point deficit in the last 10 minutes to win 86-82—with the marvelous Oscar Robertson scoring 22 of his team's last 26 points.

A reporter, arriving at the Cincinnati locker room, met Mike Mendenhall, who told him, "There's going to be a big fight in there in a minute."

"What!" the reporter screamed.

"Yeah. A fight to see who carries Oscar's bag."

HE CAN'T MISS

With 12 seconds to go and the Knickerbockers leading by 3 points, the Celtics' great center, Bill Russell, was awarded two free throws. Admittedly the worst foul shooter in the pro game, Russell converted his first shot. Then, as good strategy dictated, he deliberately tried to miss the second

shot to give his team a chance to score the tying basket. Alas,
the ball smacked the backboard and fell into the basket.

"What happened, Bill?" asked a well-wisher after the
game. "How come you made that second foul shot?"

"I guess I choked up," grinned Russell.

THE LOST CHORD

All through the basketball game, on every single play,
the Loyal Rooter had cheered his team to victory. Hoarser
and hoarser he grew until finally he whispered to the man
beside him, "What d'ya know—I've lost my voice."

"Don't worry," was the tart reply, "you'll find it in my
left ear!"

SAY IT WITHOUT MUSIC

Adolph Rupp tells visitors at Kentucky that the Coliseum
is a War Memorial and not a basketball arena. But there
was the afternoon his varsity took the floor and found an
official running up to them.

"You can't practice here," he said. "Arthur Rubinstein
is rehearsing for a piano concert and must have silence."

"Nonsense!" roared the great Wildcat coach. "Rubinstein
can play tonight and miss 100 notes and nobody in the
audience will know the difference. But let one of my
players miss a shot tomorrow night and the whole world
will hear about it. We're gonna practice."

PLAYING IT COUSY

The ardent Piston rooter was trying to disparage Bob Cousy.
"Sure he can pass," he admitted. "But when he doesn't have
the ball, he just stands around."

"Yeah, that's his weakness all right," replied the Celtic booster with a straight face. "He can't score without the ball."

FIGHTING IRISH

Pin-point penmanship by Bill Roeder, New York *World Telegram and Sun* sports columnist, in sizing up the Notre Dame basketball team: "Don't laugh them off on their record. They have one very good boy and, of course, they're Notre Dame. We hate to bet against them in checkers, let alone something you can use your elbows in."

HEARING AID

In a N.Y. Knickerbocker practice scrimmage, "Tricky" Dick McGuire was giving the veteran Carl Braun a hard time with his perpetual motion fast breaking, faking, feinting, stop-and-going.

Finally the panting Braun raised a weary hand. "Come on, Dick," he pleaded. "Take it easy on an old man."

"Carl," grinned McGuire, "I can see your lips moving, but I've turned off my hearing aid."

SCARLET LETTER

"Is your All-American, Bronko Birdbrain, as dumb as they say?" inquired a not too tactful sportswriter.

The coach remained undisturbed. "I'll say he is," he answered calmly. "When he got his letter at the annual banquet last year, I had to read it to him!"

COACH RIDE

Complaining about a tough train trip coming up, Mendy

Rudolph, crack NBA ref, grumbled, "I think I'll fly to Boston tomorrow. I'm not going to ride a coach all night."

"Why not?" snapped a nearby reporter. "Don't the coaches ride you all night?"

RAY THAT DOESN'T SHINE

Watching skinny Ray Felix, the 6-11 N. Y. Knickerbocker center, being tossed around under the basket like a kite in a tornado, a sportswriter murmured, "There's the only player I've ever seen who's 6 feet 11 inches *small*."

COFFEE BREAK

When Ben Kerner was operating the Hawks in Milwaukee, he couldn't get the fans out. During a big coffee shortage, with the stuff selling at $1.15 a pound, a Hawk fan gave Ben 1,000 pounds of coffee. The Hawk owner promptly offered his female fans a pound of coffee with every $1 ticket to the next game. Only 400 women availed themselves of this generous offer—leaving Ben with 600 pounds of coffee.

Danny Biasone, the Syracuse Nats nabob, wasn't surprised. "You should have advertised," he said, "that they didn't have to stay to watch the game."

FEUD FUEL

Off the court, Phog Allen (Kansas) and Sparky Stalcup (Missouri) were buddy-buddies. On the hardwood, they carried on a deadly feud. During a coaches' convention, a reporter noticed Stalcup with his arms draped around the Jayhawk mentor. The word flew around until it got back to the Missouri coach.

"Look," he barked, "anytime you see me with my arm around Phog you can bet it's in self-defense."

COACH COOLER

In his great years at Pittsburgh, Doc Carlson was famed for his dramatic behavior on the bench. Playing against West Virginia one night, he became incensed at the referee. After every other call, he'd throw his arms up and yell, "That burns me up!"

After the ninth or tenth shout, a Mountaineer fan couldn't take it any longer. He picked up the water bucket and emptied it over Carlson. "That," he roared, "should cool you off."

L'AMOUR TOUJOURS

The sweet little thing snuggled up to the veteran Alabama forward. "Promise me," she cooed, "that you'll think of me always."

"I'll try, dear," the forward answered, "but I cannot promise. Occasionally I might wonder if we'll ever beat Kentucky."

BLIND MAN'S BLUFF

Unhappy with the ref's interpretation of several rules, the Illinois coach, Harry Combes, invited him to stop by his office at the half and read up on the rule book.

"That isn't necessary," replied the ref, reaching for his hip pocket, "I carry my own with me at all times."

Combes reached for the ref's rule book, thumbed through a few pages, then returned it. "I just wanted to see," he said, "if it was printed in Braille."

BOO-BOO

Having run into a wild crowd that evening, referee Hagan Anderson picked up his wife and told her it might be better if she stayed away from the games to which he was assigned.

"After all," he said, "it must have been pretty embarrassing to you when everyone around you stood up and booed me."

"It wasn't so bad," she replied. "I also stood up and booed."

FROM BETTER TO WORSE

When Wilt Chamberlain wore the Crimson and Blue of Kansas, the Jayhawk coach, Dick Harp, would occasionally bench him for long periods in order to keep the score down.

Against the Big Eight cellar-dwellers one night, Harp benched Chamberlain and the opponents brought the score to 65-57 in the closing moments. In the opponents' cheering section, a young lady turned to her escort and beamed, "We're doing all right, huh?"

"Yeah, but I hope we don't do any better," sighed the boy friend, "or they'll send in Chamberlain."

OUT ON A LIMB

The coach had just finished briefing his club on what to expect the following Saturday. "Now, boys," he concluded, "what do you do when Bull Hercules gets the ball and starts driving over the middle?"

"Climb a tree!" immediately chorused the three middle linemen.

The coach played it straight. "But Bull can climb trees, too."

"Not this tree, Coach," snapped the team wit. "It would be shaking too much!"

WAVE THE WHITE SHIRT

A freshman at Senn H. S., Chicago, was issued a complete basketball outfit including a green jersey and a white jersey. The boy looked puzzled.

"Coach," he said, "I don't want to seem dumb. But why two shirts?"

"One shirt is for home and the other is for away," replied the coach.

Next day the kid returned and said, "My Ma wants to know why I have to wear the white shirt at home."

SHOOTING FOR THE STARS

Five-year-old Jimmy had been taught that Sunday is not a day for play, and his mother was horrified one Sunday morning to find him practicing pivot shots on the basket in the back yard.

"Jimmy," she scolded, "don't you know it's wicked to play ball on Sundays?"

"Oh, that's all right, mother," he replied calmly. "This isn't pleasure. I'm practicing shooting against Bill Russell!"

MILK OF HUMAN KINDNESS

The faculty at the U. of Utah are not allowed to smoke. So the nervous basketball coach, Jack Gardner, swallows milk during a game. Before one of the Ute's big games two seasons ago, an admirer wired that he was sending him a 50¢ piece to pay his milk bill for the game.

Gardner promptly wired back: "Please send another four bits. This is a two-quart game."

HAVING A BALL

Ben Kerner, owner of the St. Louis Hawks, stopped the 1956 annual draft meeting of the NBA cold when he picked Darrell Floyd, the Furman shooting whiz. Frank Selvy, the other Furman shooting whiz, was also a Hawk, and Kerner announced dramatically, "Selvy and Floyd—how about that?"

"You'll need three basketballs!" another owner shot back.

WELL DONE

"I'm fed up with rookies and green kids," another coach complained to Red Holzman, Hawk mentor. "Can't you give me a finished ball player?"

"I've got two who are all finished," rejoined Red. "Which do you want?"

HE WON'T TALK

At the draft meeting, Red Auerbach, Celtics' coach, claimed that he intended to be completely cooperative about maintaining the amateur status of his draft choices, Bill Russell and K. C. Jones, who had just been selected for the Olympic team.

"I won't even talk to them until after the Olympics," promised Red.

"Do you know whether Jones is due for military service soon?" he was asked.

"Last time I spoke to him, he said he was 1-A," replied Auerbach.

RUSSELL OF SPRING

When 6-10 Bill Russell and 7-0 Ray Felix mixed it up

under the boards one night, the crowd was treated to an amazing display of fisticuffs. Russell uncorked a sudden left hook and Felix went down and out.

Felix's teammate, Sweets Clifton, was disgusted. "Ray," he snapped, "you can't even lick a little guy."

PERFECTLY FRANK

'Tis always a pleasure to open the hoop season with a neat lay-up by Frank McGuire. The North Carolina curator of hooks and jumpers never misses with his forensic shot.

A refreshingly candid gentleman, Frank makes no bones about his predilection for New York City ball-players. He permits a lot of free-wheeling in his offense, and he believes the big-city kids have a natural flair for it.

"They're practically weaned on it," he declares. "You've got to remember that about 18,000 New York cab drivers set out every morning with just one idea in mind—to get themselves a pedestrian. To survive his childhood, the city kid's got to perfect his sudden stops and starts, reversing, side-stepping, dodging, and changes of direction.

"And if he makes the subway in one piece, he gets another half hour or so of wonderful practice on ducking, elbowing, boxing out, and commando in-fighting.

"By the time I get him, he's the slipperiest little bugger you ever saw!"

STRIKE UP THE BAND

The Moscow State Symphony Orchestra drew a crowd of 13,000 to its concert at Madison Square Garden.

"Look at this," someone said. "They draw better than the Knicks."

"Why shouldn't they?" dryly remarked his companion.
"They play a lot better."

SPEED DEMON

The team bus was careening along at 100 miles an hour,
and some of the players began sweating. Finally, one of
them tapped the coach, who was driving, on the arm.
"Coach," he said, "don't you think we're going too fast?"

"Nothing to worry about," retorted the coach. "The
Lord is riding with us."

"Maybe so, Coach," insisted the player. "But if He didn't
get on at Tiflin, He sure as hell hasn't had time since!"

HOT SHOT

When Larry Killick, the former star college and pro basket-
baller, toured the world with the Syracuse Nats the past
summer, he conducted a series of clinics on the fundamentals. At one of these seminars in Cairo, Egypt, he had
Johnny Kerr, the ex-Illinois great, demonstrate the niceties
of the one-hand push shot.

Johnny started from the corner—and hit. Then he proceeded around the horn—and his hand remained as hot as
a dragon's breath. The crowd *oohed* and *ahhed* as Johnny
kept sinking shot after shot. On his fourth goal, one of the
cords holding the net to the ring snapped. His fifth goal
snapped cord No. 2 and his sixth goal severed cord No. 3.
On his seventh consecutive basket, the net fell to the ground.
Johnny had literally shot the net off the basket!

Amid an awed silence, the big red-headed Nat walked
slowly over to the net and picked it up daintily between
thumb and forefinger. Holding it up for the crowd to see,

he casually asked:

"Any questions?"

FACE TO FACE

During one of his basketball games, Coach George Hamric of Caledonia, Ohio, noticed an opponent face-guarding one of his players. Hamric called time and beckoned to one of the officials.

"What about that face-guarding?" he demanded.

"You mean the one down at that end?" said the ref, pointing to the opposite end of the floor.

"Yes, that's the one," snapped Hamric.

"I never saw it," replied the ref.

OFFICIAL SQUAWK

The fabulous Ernie Quigley used to divide his officiating time between baseball and basketball. One night he worked a game in one of those small gyms surrounded by a balcony. The noise was terrific and suddenly Quig blew his whistle.

"There's entirely too much officiating up there in the balcony," he stormed.

Silence ensued for a moment, then came a loud, clear reply:

"Yeah, and too little on the floor!"

FIBBER McGEE

The kid was being interviewed by the coach for a basketball scholarship at the state university.

"How's your outside shot?" asked the coach.

"Deadly."

"How are you on the inside?"

"My jump shot is the greatest. I've got a tremendous change of direction, and can hook with either hand."

"What about your defense?"

"The best. Nobody has ever scored in double figures against me."

"Can you run?"

"I'm so fast I can get the rebound, pass it out, and then lead the fast break."

The coach shook his head. "Do you mean you haven't a single weakness?"

"Oh yes I have," admitted the boy cheerfully. "I tell lies."

PEN PALS

After Illinois snuffed out the fabulous San Francisco 60-game winning streak with ridiculous ease, 62-33, the A.P. tartly reported that "Woolpert (Don coach) kept the door of Frisco's dressing room locked for 15 minutes. But the Dons shouldn't have minded. The Illini had kept them locked up for 40 minutes."

MALICE IN WONDERLAND

The player complained bitterly to the ref. "That big guy deliberately threw an elbow into my face and you didn't call it."

The referee, who had gone to law school, listened patiently and unbelievingly. When the kid had finished, he said, "Do you claim that Shaw hit you with malice aforethought?"

"I didn't say that, Ref," the kid snapped. "I said he hit me with an elbow."

KOPPETT KORNER

Crack sports columnist Leonard Koppett of the *N. Y. Post,* a true hook aficionado, has compiled a brief basketball player's dictionary that hits for double figures in the funnybone league:

Team player—a player who passes the ball to me.

Ball hog—a player who wants me to pass the ball to him.

Monster—a player half an inch or more taller than me.

Little man—a player shorter than me.

Referee—a blind idiot with an unreasoning hatred of me.

Defensive star—a player who can't shoot.

Playmaker—everybody's friend (with a 2.4 average).

Bad pass—a ball that I fumble.

Fumble—another player's muff of my perfect pass.

Switch—what you holler on defense when you have no idea where your man went.

Help out—when I leave my man unguarded to get in the way of my teammate guarding the pivot man.

Clog the middle—two players helping out at once.

Good shot—any shot I can get off.

Bad shot—shot taken by a teammate.

Crazy shot—basket made by the man I'm guarding.

Cry-baby—opposing player who complains to referees.

Fighter—teammate who complains to referees.

Jump ball—holding foul by the defense that the ref didn't call.

Defensive holding—obvious jump ball.

Traveling violation—the ref's way of getting even.

Defense—how's that again?

CAGE-ILY SPEAKING

Change of Direction—the first move after spotting a bill collector.

Referee—a lunatic who breathes into whistles.

Coach—a tormented psychotic who asks you to do the impossible.

Give-and-Go—turning in a blank exam paper and rushing for the door.

Splitting the Post—Abe Lincoln's boyhood chores.

Man-to-Man—the kind of talk nobody has with Junior any more.

Foul Shot—jabbing the knife into the Thanksgiving turkey.

Fast Break—the first 9-course dinner after a 7-day diet.

Reverse English—explaining your team's chances before the season.

Bank Shot—hitting the Corn Exchange for that second mortgage.

Traveling—what losing coaches do a lot of.

Double Dribble—a baby with an over-active salivary gland.

3-Second Rule—"unhand my daughter and get out of the parlor..."

10-Second Rule—"and don't slam the door behind you."

Four-Man Weave—the sportwriters' trek homeward after the annual banquet.

Figure-of-8—the human form after a 12-course Italian dinner.

Pick-Off—worrying the scab off a wounded patella.

Blocking Out—what your chapeau needs after the state final play-off.

Deliberate Offense—what mothers-in-law generally give.

Sharp Cut—Xmas present in the losing coach's salary.

Rebounding—a jilted lover in search of a warm smile.

Switch—change of subject when you ask the principal for a raise.

Slide—when the material runs out, you go into it.

Cold Night—when the girl friend says goodbye at the gate.

Clearing Out an Area—climbing out the back window when the hotel bill comes due.

Circulation Drill—push-ups on a wintry morning while waiting for the janitor to fix the radiator.

Cross-Court Pass—a leer at the pretty blonde on the other side of the net.

Clog the Middle—over-eat.

Bounce Pass—what happens to personal checks received from strangers.

Delayed Offense—that flush of anger two days later.

Natural Shooter—a fellow who can roll 7's and 11's while standing on his ear.

Shooting Chart—chicken tracks made by tormented student managers.

Scissoring—the therapeutic activity of losing coaches who wind up in insane asylums.

Inside Screen—the barrier you try to get by on your first date.

Staleness—the condition of the coach's after-dinner jokes.

Tournament Play—where the last touch of sanity vanishes.

Homer—what every official is to the losing coach.

Hook Pass—a kleptomaniac's major diversion.

Free Throw—the fourth round at the neighborhood pub.

Three-Lane Break—charge of the hot rods when the traffic light turns green.

Outlet Pass—a phony comp that gets you thrown out of the arena.

THE OLD GLIB-AND-GO

By Fred Price, *Coach, Trenton (N. J.) Central H. S.*

Casey Stengel has no monopoly on double-talk. Once the basketball season rolls around, friends, fans, reporters, and other well-wishers bombard hoop coaches with questions about their teams. For reasons best known to us coaches, most answers take the form of stock phrases or sentences, usually cloaking our true feelings. Following is a list of these answers, with accompanying translations, which John Q. Public will either hear or read during the course of the hardwood season:

STATEMENT: "I'm junking the weave for a single-pivot next year."

TRANSLATION: *A 6:7 transfer enrolled during the summer.*

STATEMENT: "We may get a bit of help from our reserves."

TRANSLATION: *His JV team was 24-1 last season.*

STATEMENT: "We've juggled the schedule to make it more attractive."

TRANSLATION: *Some of the tougher opponents have been dropped.*

STATEMENT: "I hope we can rebound better this season."

TRANSLATION: *His starting five will average 6:3.*

STATEMENT: "To be a great player, you must always *think* basketball."

TRANSLATION: *He's worried because three regulars are going steady.*

STATEMENT: "Our fans will see a fighting, hustling ball club."

TRANSLATION: *He lost three All-County players through graduation.*

STATEMENT: "The play patterns we devised are beginning to click."

TRANSLATION: *Four of the first five are shooting above 40%.*

STATEMENT: "If my center keeps practicing, he can make All-State."

TRANSLATION: *The boy is thinking about a part-time job.*

STATEMENT: "I hope to do much more scouting this year."

TRANSLATION: *He's been able to get expense money for his wife.*

STATEMENT: "We hope to be stronger in the backcourt."

TRANSLATION: *Both guards were honorable mention All-Staters.*

STATEMENT: "Competition is so keen, we cut several good prospects."

TRANSLATION: *Why doesn't the school buy more than 12 game uniforms?*

STATEMENT: "It was purely a judgment call on his part."

TRANSLATION: *He'll never referee another home game for us.*

STATEMENT: "We will be working on basic ball-handling tomorrow."

TRANSLATION: *The opponents' pressing tactics broke the game wide open.*

STATEMENT: "Defense will be a major factor in tonight's game."

TRANSLATION: *If we can't hold their leading scorer, we're done.*

STATEMENT: "Circumstances often dictate the type defense to use."

TRANSLATION: *In this bandbox, we expect a full-court press all game.*

STATEMENT: "The away games this year will give us needed experience."

TRANSLATION: *He's hoping for an even split on the road.*

STATEMENT: "The boy's family talks nothing but basketball."

TRANSLATION: *The coach is being second-guessed for not playing their son more often.*

III

SLIDERS AND SCREWBALLS

MOANING THE BLUES

Walker Cooper was the Cardinals catcher when Augie Guglielmo made his first appearance as a National League arbiter.

When he heard Guglielmo's name mentioned as an umpire, Cooper exclaimed, "Guglielmo, Passarella, Pinelli, Dascoli, Donatelli, Paparella!" Then, turning to Guglielmo, he asked with a grin, "Does every Italian get a blue suit the moment he steps off the boat?"

BASE ON BALLS

The first time up Ted Williams tripled. Second time he put one over the wall. Then he slugged a pair of doubles. Next time up he walked on four pitches.

Catcher Sherm Lollar turned to the ump and growled, "You sure put him on base that time."

"Maybe I did," agreed the man in blue. "But at least I held him to one base."

FRISCH-LY LAID EGG

Thumbed out of the ball game, the irrepressible Frankie Frisch demanded to know the reason.

"Because you can't call me a lugger-head," snarled Umpire Dusty Boggess.

"Just what I thought," shouted Frisch. "You're deaf as well as blind. I didn't call you lugger-head. I called you blubber-head!"

THE SOFT SELL

Former American League ump, Red Jones, was working a

prison game. The star of the jailhouse nine was an immense fellow with a real mean look in his eye, and Jones decided it would be judicious to soften him up.

"What are you in for?" he asked in a friendly manner.

"For killing a guy about twice your size," leered the inmate.

SMACK IN THE KISSER

Rocky Bridges, who admits he's a regular on the big league All-Ugly team, was hit in the face by a pitched ball. He lay in a daze as the trainer rushed out to him.

"Talk to me," pleaded the trainer, who believed Rocky was seriously hurt.

Bridges slowly raised his head. "George," he asked, "will this spoil my movie career?"

BEWILDERED BEGINNING

After 21 years in baseball, the Dodgers' great little shortstop, Pee Wee Reese, retired to the coaching lines in 1959. Asked about the difficulty of making the transition from player to coach, Pee Wee replied:

"I felt like a mosquito in a nudist colony. I didn't know where to begin."

BEHIND EVERY MAN

It's generally agreed that Dick Stuart of the Pirates is the worst fielding first baseman since Zeke Bonura. "Believe me," he told a writer, "getting married was the greatest thing that ever happened to me. It really straightened me out. Behind every successful man stands a good woman."

"With a first baseman's mitt?" queried the writer.

KLEM CLINCHER

Frankie Frisch was telling the late Bill Klem it was a cinch
to umpire. "All you have to do is jerk your right arm in a
circle and roar, 'Yer-r-r-r ow-w-wit!' I could do that all
day," concluded Frankie.

"No, you couldn't," contradicted Klem. "Supposin' the
runner was safe?"

SKOWRON CLEANS UP

Following a tremendous year at Kansas City, Bill Skowron
was called up by the Yankees in 1954. "What are Skowron's
chances for sticking?" asked a reporter of Casey Stengel.

"He can't miss," snorted the Perfesser. "Why, that feller
led the American Association in everything but stolen
towels."

LONG WAY OFF

Having implored his manager, Harry Craft, for a chance
to start, the rookie hurler promptly walked the first four
batters, was tagged for three straight hits, uncorked three
wild pitches, then walked three more men before Manager
Craft could get out there and take him away.

"Well," snarled Craft, as they walked back to the dugout, "what have you got to say for yourself?"

"Maybe I was a little off today," alibied the rookie.

"But not as far off as you'll be tomorrow," growled the
manager.

IN A MINOR KEY

In the days of the parsimonious Clark Griffith, a youngster
showed up at a Washington try-out school and proceeded

to dazzle one and all with a dazzling fast ball and curve. The Senator owner offered him a $500 bonus to sign a contract. The kid refused. Griffith then upped his offer to $750. The lad's enthusiasm remained restrained. Finally the Senator owner said he'd pay $1,000, but that was his final bid.

"Mr. Griffith," said the boy coolly, "if that's all you can offer, I'd rather wait and sign with a major league team."

THREE-WAY HITTER

Asked for an appraisal of a rookie with whom he had played in the minors, the Pirates' Dick Stuart had a ready answer. "This fellow has it over Mickey Mantle in at least one respect. Mickey hits two ways; this fellow hits *three*—left-handed, right-handed, and seldom."

BLACK-OUT

The two hill-billy rookies, aboard a train for the first time in their lives and positively awed by it, bought a basket of fruit at the first stop. Though neither had ever seen an avocado before, one of them started bringing it to his mouth —just as the train catapulted into a tunnel.

As everything went black, the kid with the avocado in his hand suddenly shouted:

"Jeb, if you ain't bit into that thing yet, don't. I just did —and I'm going blind."

SATCH SEES RED

Upon entering the major leagues in 1948, the fabulous Satchel Paige was upset by a newspaper story claiming he owned a big red car with "Satchel Paige, World's Greatest Pitcher" embossed on the door.

"That story ain't true," Satch complained to his manager. "I never owned a red car—it's maroon."

WHAT'S IN A NAME

Called out at second base, Eddie Stanky let off some steam at the ump and was promptly heaved out of the game. That brought his manager, the ebullient Leo Durocher, onto the scene.

"Whadja throw him out of the game for?" the Lip demanded.

"Because," roared the umpire, "he said I was blind and stupid and he called me a dirty name."

"Leave off the dirty name," roared the Lip right back, "and just how wrong was he?"

VERY PRIVATE EYE

Casey Stengel was something of a playboy back in his Giant days. On occasion, manager John McGraw would put a detective on his tail. Stengel paired off with Irish Meusel for extra-curricular outings, and they led the private eye a merry chase.

Finally Casey became enraged. "I'm particular," he informed McGraw. "From now on I don't want to share a detective with anybody."

X MARKS THE SPOT

To kill time, a group of Los Angeles Dodgers were playing the old guessing game, with orchestra or band leaders as the category. Somebody would give the initials and the others would try to guess his identity.

"E. C.," said Gino Cimoli.

"Eddie Condon," guessed Vin Scully.

"No."

"Earl Conroy," said Pee Wee Reese.

"Nope."

The players wrestled with the problem for about five minutes and finally gave up.

"Exavier Cugat," beamed Cimoli.

MONUMENTAL PEG

In Albie Pearson's first game in the Yankee Stadium, Mickey Mantle clouted a ball behind the monuments in deep center. Albie scurried behind the monuments and was lost from view for several seconds while frantically scrambling for the ball. He finally retrieved it and threw to shortstop Rocky Bridges, but much too late to prevent Mickey from circling the bases.

Bridges walked over to Albie and shook his head: "I waited so long out there I thought Miller Huggins was going to throw me the ball."

HAPPEN-STANCE

Manager Casey Stengel has always been puzzled about Yogi Berra's innumerable foul-ball home runs. "He musta missed out on at least 30 homers last season. Each time at the last second the ball curved foul."

In due course, the eminent Perfesser concluded that it was a matter of stance. Berra had been standing improperly. So in spring training he changed the position of Berra's feet.

"How did it work out?" inquired a scribe.

"Why, you seen how remarkable it works," retorted Stengel. "Now Berra ain't even hitting any fouls."

HISTORICAL BASEBALL LINGO

"If Men in History Had Spoken Like Baseball Managers"

is the title of a most witty Joe Falls' column in the Detroit *Times*:

George Washington: Give me another left-handed oarsman and I'll get across the Delaware.

Jesse James: I'd like to see my guys steal more often this year.

Steve Brodie: The important thing is to get a big jump.

Thomas Jefferson: I'm sure the purchase of Louisiana is going to help us.

Abraham Lincoln: Boy, are we in a slump! When was the last time we made four scores—seven years ago?

Teddy Roosevelt: You can have your "holler" guys. Give me some one who speaks softly and carries a big stick.

Robert E. Lee: I think the Yankees can be beaten.

Stephen Foster: I like to see someone who can hum, especially if he's got the right pitch.

Thomas Edison: We could use some more power.

Chief Justice Warren: Our bench is stronger than ever.

Ulysses S. Grant: Of course, it's important to win in the South.

Nathan Hale: Actually I don't think I'd care to go out on a limb.

A COUPLE OF BREAKS

At the 1959 baseball writers dinner in New York City, Mayor Bob Wagner smote a four-bagger with the bases full. "Branch Rickey made two great contributions to baseball," noted hizzoner. "He broke the color line in Brooklyn, and the treasury in Pittsburgh."

HEAVEN ONLY KNOWS

The Senators had lost 18 straight back at the turn of the century, and were trailing in Detroit, 1-0, when the skies blackened. Then Washington tallied five times. But before Manager Joe Cantillon could rush the game through, the storm broke and washed out the inning—leaving his team with its 19th defeat.

Still in uniform, the players ran for their horse-drawn bus. As the last player climbed aboard, a bolt of lightning struck, killing both horses. Cantillon lifted his clenched hands to the skies.

"Oh, Lord," he prayed. "What kind of justice is there in heaven that strikes these poor dumb creatures dead and lets these miserable, unspeakable vegetables sit there alive?"

NOTHING BUT A PRAYER

When Johnny Nee was scouting for the Yankees in the days of Colonel Jake Ruppert, he once signed a rookie prospect who happened to be a clergyman on the side. He paid the kid $500, but the boy never reported.

The Colonel was furious. "Nee," he roared, "you've squandered $500. What do I get for it?"

"Good will, Colonel," soothed the scout. "Just think—*he'll pray for you!*"

POSITION IS EVERYTHING

Hank Aaron was taking batting practice in Shibe Park. He belted the first ball over 400 feet into the upper left-center seats, where a fan made a fine bare-handed catch. A moment later Henry belted another ball into the same sector, where the same fan again plucked the ball out of the air —amid a tremendous cheer.

Aaron grinned: "That guy is sure playing me right."

CALLING ALL ELEPHANTS

Umpire Ed Runge was needling Billy Martin about his

.220 batting average. "Boy, you're a miserable hitter these days. Why, if somebody threw you an *elephant,* you couldn't hit it."

"Ed," knifed back Martin, "if somebody threw me an elephant, you couldn't *call* it."

SPRINT TIME

The Phillies' pitching coach, Tom Ferrick, likes to run his charges' legs off. One afternoon he noticed pitcher Art Fowler leaning against the centerfield fence, panting like a marathon runner crossing the tape.

"What's the matter, Art?" he drawled. "Feeling a bit tired? You know you gotta keep running if you want to have a big year."

"Heck," groaned Fowler. "If running were so important, Jesse Owens would be a 20-game winner."

HITTING THE SNAIL ON THE HEAD

Shaggy Snail Story from Joe Wilmot of the *San Francisco Chronicle*: "Nine snails got together and formed a baseball team. Next day their first pieces of equipment arrived—nine Louisville Sluggards."

FOWLER BALL

Art Fowler was to be the Redleg starter the day his old buddy, Glen Gorbous, returned to Crosley Field as a Phillie. As Glen passed the Redleg dugout, Fowler yelled, "You'd better stay loose today, Glen, because I'm gonna put one down your ear."

"Impossible," dead-panned Gorbous.

"You don't think I can hit you with a pitch?" yelled the scornful Fowler.

"Nope," grinned Gorbous, "because I'm going to be sitting on the bench."

A GOOD PITCH

Lefty Gomez was clouted for a tremendous home run in a game against the White Sox. Returning to the dugout, he was accosted by his manager, Joe McCarthy.

"Was that a good pitch he hit?" McCarthy gritted.

Gomez looked his skipper square in the eye. "It was a beauty," he enthused. "Did you see him hit the cover off it?"

BIG DISH

Several evenings after the Russians launched a rocket to the moon, the Indians' pitching coach, Mel Harder, and sportswriter Frank Gibbons were standing on a street corner. Harder looked up at the big moon hanging in the sky.

"It's a lot bigger than home plate," he observed. "How could they possibly miss it?"

PEARLY OBSERVATION

Three ministers who had led exemplary lives arrived at the Pearly Gates at the same time—and were surprised to have St. Peter ask them to wait in the outer lobby while he briefly chatted with another new arrival, a southpaw pitcher famous for his wildness.

St. Peter waved in the pitcher with a flourish, then took his time interviewing the three clergymen. Asked why a layman should get into the Promised Land before the worthy three, St. Peter logically pointed out:

"Why, that man has scared the devil out of far more people than you have!"

PARKER ROLLS

Before the historic Braves-Dodgers playoff last October, Dan Parker, the crack syndicated sports columnist, threw a delightful fast ball at one of his pet targets, Dodger President Walter O'Malley:

"If three games are required to break the tie and let the World Series proceed, two days behind schedule, Walter the Wildflower of Smogville will lose the Sunday date at his makeshift ball park in the Coliseum, which he has been counting upon to produce the largest receipts ever for a World Series game. Already suffering from the Brooklyn ailment, fallen archeries, from toting his gold to the bank every day, Walter could develop hardening of the artilleries from this setback. Meantime, his Flatbush idolators are on the verge of dementia peacocks not to mention delirious trimmings, worrying that Walter won't become a billionaire."

PAINLESS SURGERY

Manager Fred Haney is a thoughtful gent who tries to remove a pitcher as painlessly as possible. One afternoon, after his pitcher had been blasted for a half dozen hits in a row, Fred went out to give him the rest of the day off.

"But Mr. Haney," protested the pitcher, "they were all freak hits. I just haven't been getting the breaks."

"I know, son," consoled Haney. "I don't think the fellow coming in will be any better. I'm just hoping he'll be a little luckier."

GIVE THE KID A HAND

During the regime of John McGraw, the Giants brought

up a rookie whom they immediately installed in the outfield. A ball was hit past him and he lost his glove while fielding it. Then, to everyone's amazement, he ran back and picked up the glove before retrieving the ball—while the batter scampered around the bases.

When the rookie returned to the dugout at the end of the inning, McGraw was waiting on the steps. "Can you tell me why you ran after your glove instead of the ball?" roared Little Napoleon.

"Mr. McGraw," replied the rookie in an injured tone, "I had to find out what hand to throw with, didn't I?"

LAST CALL

The vituperative woman in the box seat behind third base kept hurling a stream of abuse at Dick Elkind, then catching for Hutchinson. At a critical moment in the game, Dick grounded out and the witch in the box really let him have it.

"You stupid, ugly ape, who ever told you you could play ball!"

Elkind turned, looked at her for a moment, then yelled loudly and clearly, "Honey, that's not what you called me up in the hotel room last night."

BLIND-MAN'S BLUFF

One of the few managers who ever stood up to general manager Frank (Trader) Lane was Black Jack Onslow. One day Lane charged Onslow and roared, "I could coach third base blindfolded better than you did this afternoon."

The hard-bitten Onslow jawed right back, "I don't doubt it. You do everything else blindfolded."

FANNING BEE

When the Detroit Tiger wit, Rocky Bridges, heard that the

White Sox's Bill Veeck planned to air-condition Comiskey Park, he promptly cracked, "I understand that Veeck is gonna try to put a fan in every seat."

VALUABLE LESSON

Back in his Dodger days, Jackie Robinson had a bitter feud with the late Mike Gaven. One night when the sportswriter entered the dugout, Jackie took out after him.

"You writers are always wrong, always wrong," Robinson shrilled.

Gaven looked him up and down, then murmured, "You mean like when we voted you the Most Valuable Player last year?"

EDUCATION ON THE FLY

Jim Whatley, U. of Georgia baseball mentor, went to school (Alabama) with Mel Allen, the famous announcer.

"As a freshman outfielder," vouchsafes Jim, "Mel would run in on a fly ball shouting, 'I got it,' then drop the ball. But Mel majored in English. When he was a senior, and better educated, Mel would run in on a foul ball shouting, 'I *have* it!'—then drop it."

SMART PITCH

Clark Griffith was pitching against the Phillies in the last half of the ninth. Though there were two out, the tying run was on second and at bat was the fearful Delahanty with the even more fearful Lajoie on deck.

Griffith eyed Delahanty up and down, then looked at Lajoie. He shuffled his feet, rubbed up the ball, twitched his cap. Then he paced around the mound. Finally he walked Delahanty and pitched to Lajoie, who became the victim of a spectacular catch.

As Griffith walked to the clubhouse, he was accosted by the umpire. "What in the world were you thinking about, passing Delahanty to get to Lajoie?" asked the arbiter.

"I noticed," replied the pitcher, "that Delahanty was looking at the fences while Lajoie was looking at the infield set-up. I decided to pick the guy with the least ambitious look."

BIRD-BATH

Milwaukee's general manager, Johnny McHale, claims that the Braves' Humberto Robinson, who stands 6-1 but weighs only 148 pounds, is "so skinny he can take a bath in a double-barreled shotgun."

RUBBER DUB-DUB

Contemplating a change in the dimensions of the pitching rubber, the American League asked the advice of its greatest pitcher, Lefty Gomez.

"It makes no difference to me," shrugged Gomez.

"But it should," insisted one of the club presidents. "After all, your livelihood depends on where you stand on the pitching rubber."

"What do I care?" retorted Gomez. "I never fooled anyone with my feet."

WATER UNDER THE BRIDGES

Rocky Bridges, the Tigers' wit, always likes to stroll through Michigan Avenue's Skid Row in Detroit. As he explains it, "It's good for me. I run into a lot of old ball players who forgot to swing on that 3-and-2 pitch."

Asked why he's the first one in the clubhouse and the last one out, Rocky replied, "I like to chew, spit and lie."

COMING AND GOING

Back in the days of the Yankees' Murderers' Row, Babe Ruth was known as a playboy while Lou Gehrig personified the All-American Boy.

Everyone who knew them was always asked if it was true they didn't get along. The famous umpire, Harry Geisel, would always answer the question in this fashion:

"If you come down to the hotel any night about 10:30, you'll always see them together. You'll see Lou comin' in and the Babe goin' out."

COMMERCIAL NOTE

After retiring from the Yankees, Gerry Coleman confined his TV appearances to commercials. His little nephew, who had never seen him play ball, kept asking, "Did you really play for the Yankees?"

"Certainly," Coleman replied. "Why do you ask?"

"Well, everytime I see you on TV, you're either shaving or smoking."

SOBRIETY DOESN'T PAY

Somewhat the worse for wear after an all-night stand on the town, Doc Cramer wobbled into the ballpark and found his way to the outfield.

The first time up, he doubled in two runs.

The second time at bat, he tripled off the center-field wall.

The third time at the plate, he homered.

Came the ninth with the score tied and a man on third— and Cramer popped to the infield.

Manager Connie Mack shook his head, "I was afraid of what would happen when he sobered up."

SPIRIT IS WILLING

The baseball coach was selling tickets for a benefit game. He approached the local realtor, a notorious skinflint, and asked how many tickets he would like to have.

"I'm sorry I can't buy any," the gentleman answered. "I won't be able to be there. But I want you to know my spirit will be there with you."

"Good!" snapped the coach. "I have a fine selection of $1, $2, and $3 seats. Where would you like your spirit to sit?"

DOUBTING THOMAS

The dyed-in-the-wool Pittsburgh Pirate fan let out a bellow when Frank Thomas stepped to the plate. "Get that bum outta there. He couldn't hit a basketball!"

The fellow next to him tapped him on the shoulder. "Lay off Thomas," he warned, "he's a friend of mine."

"Okay," growled the loud-mouth, "but tell me, how many other bums on that team are pals of yours?"

"Well, to name a few there are Bob Friend, Dick Groat, and Dee Fondy."

"Holy cow!" groaned the fan. "Lemme outa here. You ain't gonna stop me from enjoying this game!"

JUMPING JACK

Jack Harshman, the big left-hander, was once a first baseman. Asked why he gave up infielding for the mound, he replied:

"If you don't succeed at first, try pitching."

SOURING THE VINEGAR

Vinegar Bend Mizell, the Cardinals' eccentric southpaw,

was blasted for a long homer by Willie Mays. "It was a good pitch," mumbled Mizell in the dugout, "I actually got it halfway past him."

"That's your trouble," snapped Manager Freddie Hutchison. "You think it's the first half that counts. It's the second half that's all important."

HOT DIGGITY DOG

Engrossed in one of those Giant-Dodger donnybrooks, the two rooters didn't want to march back to the refreshment stand for hot dogs. They snagged a nearby kid and told him, "Here's 60 cents. Get us two franks and buy yourself one at the same time."

The kid returned ten minutes later with 40 cents change. "Sorry," he explained, "they only had MY hot dog left."

GOLFING FEES

While managing Minneapolis one year, Tommy Heath became incensed when his slumping hitters began paying too much attention to golf. The Millers' skipper called a club meeting and announced:

"Certainly you can keep playing golf, but from now on the green fees will be 50 bucks."

THE RAINS CAME

Fred Haney is still twitted about his dark years with the hopeless Pirates. "Oh, it wasn't so bad," Haney grins. "I once remember when we lost 8 in a row. The ninth day it rained and I tossed a victory party for the players."

FAIR TRADE

Bubber Jonnard, Kansas City scout, received a letter from

an aspiring young pitcher who asked for a chance to prove himself. "I have a fast ball like an intercontinental missile, a curve that arcs like a satellite, an inshoot that looks like a profile of Jane Mansfield, and a drop that dives like the Nautilus."

"Did you bring him in for a look?" Jonnard was asked.

"I sure did," grinned Bubber. "Then I traded him to the Defense Dept. for two space cadets."

PLAYING IT SAFELY

On the day Haney received a national safety award, outfielder Jerry Lynch, in quick succession, dropped a fly ball, got hit on the head with another fly, fumbled a grounder, hit the left field wall with a throw, then tripped himself and fell flat going back for an easy fly.

At this point, Haney took him out of the game. "I had to do it, Jerry," he explained. "If I didn't, you'd have gotten killed and they'd have taken away my national safety award."

UNBROADENING TRAVEL

After graduating from Harvard, Charlie Devens reported to the Yankees carrying a suitcase plastered with travel stickers from all over the world. The great Lefty Gomez studied all the stickers carefully, then turned to Devens and said:

"Y'ever been to Newark, kid?"

FAIR HARVARD

Once a Harvard man always a Harvard man. That even applies to Howell Stevens, an old Harvardian who now covers sports for a Boston paper. He was once asked if he could contribute anything to the obituary of a Harvard alumnus who had been president of several corporations, a leading philanthropist, a pillar of society, and a noted authority on the history of naval warfare.

"Oh, him," replied Stevens, "he's the bum who got caught stealing home in the Yale game."

14-CARROT GOLD

Mrs. Carl Furillo was trying to prove helpful at the dinner table by ladling heaps of carrots onto her famous hubby's plate. "Carrots are good for your eyes, dear," she explained.

"Yes, honey," the Dodger outfielder sweetly replied. "But they'll never straighten out the curve ball."

QUICK BREAKER

Speaking of curves, there's the one about Joe Kelly, old-time Reading (Pa.) outfielder who was sold to Toronto because he couldn't hit that kind of pitch. On his way to join his new club, Kelly was stopped at the border by the immigration officials. "How long do you expect to stay in Canada?" asked one of the officials.

"Until they start throwing curves," promptly answered Joe.

DIDN'T KNOW IT WAS LOADED

When Lefty Gomez was fast-balling them for the Yankees, the coaching staff's big worry was that the unpredictable Señor wasn't concentrating enough. One afternoon the White Sox loaded the bases against him and Coach Art Fletcher immediately walked out to the mound. He wanted to make sure that Gomez was aware of the situation.

"Say, Lefty," he said, "do you know the bases are loaded?"

Gomez looked at him grimly. "Of course I do," he
snapped. "I know I'm not playing with two infields in back
of me!"

BAD HOP

Try as he might, Paul Richards couldn't get the rookie
infielder to play the ball rather than let it play him. After
the rookie cost the Orioles a ball game, Richards lost his
patience. "From now on," he snapped, "it's going to cost
you $25 every time you fail to charge a grounder."

That very afternoon, the young infielder lost the game
by playing a hopper on its second rather than first bounce.
When the kid returned to the dugout, Richards told him
"That play cost you $50."

"But you said you were going to fine me only $25," the
rookie protested.

"That was this morning," gritted Richards. "I've since
decided to make it $25 a bounce.

NO PAY FOR OVERTIME

In a late spring exhibition game, the Dodgers belted Lew
Burdette pretty badly in the first inning and Coach Billy
Herman was sent out to the mound to get him out of there.

"It's only an exhibition game," Lew protested. "Let me
stay in. I need the work."

"Sure you do," grinned second baseman Red Schoen-
dienst. "But the outfielders are getting more than they
can use."

BYRNED UP

When Tommy Byrne started out in organized baseball, he
was so wild he couldn't keep the ball in the park. One after-

noon the general manager called him into his office.

"Tommy," he said, "I'm sorry but I'm sending you to Hutchinson."

"For whom?" asked Byrne.

"For nobody," the g.m. informed him. "It's an even trade that will strengthen our ball club."

LIGHTS OUT!

In the early days of night ball, Elmer Singleton, former big leaguer, was once batting in Albany, N. Y., with a 2-and-1 count. As the pitcher wound up, the lights suddenly went out. Singleton, frightened, immediately hit the dirt. After hugging the ground for about a minute, he began feeling foolish and started getting up. Just as he did, the lights suddenly came on again.

Quite a sight greeted his eyes: Every infielder and out-fielder, even the catcher, was flat on the ground!

CAUGHT WITH HIS SHINGUARDS DOWN

On a blooper to left, burly Johnny Blatnik, then playing for Houston, tried to score from second. Behind the plate was Tiger Tappe, the Beaumont funny man. The small but tough Tiger held his ground. Just as he caught the ball, he was sent crashing against the front-row box seats. He lay there, a small quivering lump of protoplasm, as the ump came rushing up to him.

"Tappe," bellowed the ump, "if you've got that ball, that guy is out!"

"Got the ball?" moaned the catcher. "Mr. Umpire, I ain't even got my shinguards!"

COMEDY OF ERRORS

In the White Sox days of Jimmy Dykes and Zeke Bonura,

manager Dykes would always check with catcher Luke Sewell whenever Zeke, probably the worst fielding first baseman of all time, would give the one-hand salute to balls hit by first base.

Invariably after each misdemeanor, Dykes would ask Sewell, "You think he should have got it?" Luke would reply "yes" and Dykes would chew out Zeke.

Finally Sewell began to think, "Bonura won't be friendly any more if I keep this up." So the next time a ball went past first and Dykes asked, "Should he . . .?" Luke replied, "I don't think so."

Thereupon Dykes took off on Sewell. "You mean to tell me a first baseman couldn't have gotten that ball?"

"Sure," replied Sewell, "but you didn't ask me that. You asked me if Bonura could have gotten it."

THE MANAGER HAS HIS INNING

When the manager came out to the mound, the pitcher refused to leave the game. "Gee, I can handle the next hitter," he insisted. "I struck him out the first time I faced him, remember?"

The pilot shook his head sadly. "Yeah, but that was this inning!"

HEIR CONDITIONED

One of the greatest diamond raconteurs extant, Tommy Richardson, president of the Eastern League, has been slaying 'em for years with the one about a ball player named Riley, who was drowned when his fishing boat capsized. Everyone was astonished upon learning that he had left $100,000.

"To think he'd leave you that much money," intoned

Mrs. Murphy to Mrs. Riley at the wake. "Him that could nather read nor write."

"Nor schwimm, ayther," added Mrs. Riley.

SIGNAL SYSTEM

The veteran catcher walked out to the mound to discuss signals with the raw rookie hurler. "Well, son, what kind of pitches do you have?"

The brash rookie began itemizing his assortment: "I've got a fast ball, a slow ball, a great screwball, four different kinds of curves, a drop, two kinds of . . ."

"Whoa, there, boy!" interrupted the catcher. "I've got a glove on one hand and only five fingers on the other. How can I signal for so many pitches?"

"Well," snapped the rookie, "take off your shoes and use your toes."

FAR, FAR FROM HOME

National Leaguers complain that the dugouts in San Francisco are so far from the batter's box that they can't get on the plate umpires. "You have to wait till the next game," grins Duke Snider, "and give him hell at third base!"

OLE ON L. A.

T.V.'s Art Linkletter did a masterful job of emceeing the first annual baseball writers' dinner for the Los Angeles scribes on the eve of the 1958 opener.

"My tickets in the Coliseum," he said cracked, "are Seat 67, Aisle 72, Highway 99."

And about the zany driving on the car-jammed freeways out there, he said, "You can drive 15 miles on any freeway and never leave the scene of an accident."

COAT FOR CASEY

At the height of the Bernard Goldfine-vicuna coat scandal, Casey Stengel appeared before the Senate Subcommittee to testify on various aspects of big league baseball.

Later Casey bragged, "Yeah, I got that Goldfine feller off the front pages. Maybe he'll send me one of them petunia coats."

THERE'S NO TOMORROW

One afternoon Lefty Gomez's fiance, the beauteous June O'Dea, dropped in at the Stadium to see him pitch for the first time. Lefty pitched his heart out, but lost a 14-inning thriller, 1-0.

In an effort to console her spouse-to-be after the game, the musical comedy star murmured, "Never mind, honey. You'll beat 'em tomorrow."

"*Tomorrow!*" screamed Gomez. "You must have me mixed up with Iron-Man McGinnity!"

KING FOR A DAY

Witty Nellie King, former Pirate pitcher, convulsed the gathering at the Pittsburgh Dapper Dan Dinner when he got to his feet and remarked: "I'm up here to get an award as the pitcher who backed up third base the most times in 1957!"

IN THE BAG

Watching one of his pitching discoveries chucking the ball all over the lot, the veteran scout, Charlie Barrett, went out to consult with him. "What's the matter with your control?" he asked.

The rookie explained, "I'm nervous today and can't keep my hand dry."

"Here's a resin bag," replied Barrett. "It will help dry your hand."

When the kid kept bouncing the ball all over the screen, Charlie went out again. "Didn't that resin bag help?" he asked.

"Gee, I don't know," the kid answered. "I couldn't get the darn bag open!"

AMONG THE MISSING

After getting blasted for six hits and seven runs in three innings, the Tiger right-hander, Paul Foytack, explained that his fast ball didn't have that little something extra— "and when that something extra is missing, generally a lot of baseballs are too."

FEATHER DUSTER

The ubiquitous Bobo Newsom never hesitated to keep the batters uneasy and shaky up at the plate. "Did you ever deliberately knock anyone down?" he was asked.

"No, I never did," he replied with a grin. "But I recollect that the ball did."

TRADE WIND

When the much-traded Mickey McDermott was dealt away by the Yankees, he complained that Casey Stengel never gave him enough chances to pitch.

To which the Yankee skipper replied: "I notice wherever they gave McDermott enough chances to pitch, a lot of managers were fired."

TAYLOR-MADE

The Cubs went into 1958 spring training with three Taylors
—infielder Tony Taylor, catcher Sam Taylor, and pitcher
Taylor Phillips. "It figures," remarked Billy Herman.
"They can't have too many tailors for all the holes they got
in that club."

FIT TO BE TIED

Kansas City sports scribe Ed Garich agrees with owner
Arnold Johnson that the Athletics have no ties with the
Yankees. "No ties, just defeats," he says.

WHAT'S IN A NAME

A kid rushed up to the big league player and asked for his
autograph. He began fidgeting as the player wrote and
wrote. "Look, kid," observed the player, "if you want my
autograph, you gotta be patient."

The player's name? Arnold Portocarrero!

SUPPLY AND DEMAND

When the great Satchell Paige was pitching for the Indians
back in Bill Veeck's day, there were always two tickets left
at the press gate in the name of Mrs. Satchell Paige. This
intrigued Veeck since he had no idea Paige was married.
So he stopped Satch one day and asked, "Are you married,
Satch?"

To which Paige replied softly, "No sir, but I'm in great
demand."

GLASS-EYED SKIPPER

A couple of days after the great Murtaugh-Gomez-Cepeda

rhubarb, several of the sports scribes were discussing the brawl with the Giants' skipper, Bill Rigney.

"I looked at the pictures," said a writer to Rig, "and saw Murtaugh right in the middle of the ruckus. But where were you?"

"Didn't you see me?" replied Rigney with a pained expression. "I was right there in the middle."

"With the bat?" said the writer.

"No," said Rigney, "with the glasses on."

ROCKY ROAD TO SUCCESS

Early in the 1958 baseball season, Rocky Bridges, impish Senator shortstop, was scanning the statistics and noted that Bob Cerv had hit 11 homers and driven in 31 runs.

"He's off to a good start," a friend remarked.

"If I had that many homers and rbi's," cracked Rocky, "I'd call it a good year."

HOLE-Y BAT

One afternoon in Nashville, the Knoxville Smokies, having expended all their available bench strength, sent in weak-hitting Dick Coffman to pinch-hit for the only man in the league who was a worse hitter than he.

Coffman took elaborate pains to pick a stick, then walked up and took three straight strikes. Returning to the bat rack, he carefully replaced the stick and muttered, "That bat ain't got no wood in it."

LOGAN-BERRY WINE

One of the more popular after-dinner speakers among the big leaguers is Johnny Logan, the Braves' peppery shortstop. Though he has difficulty finding the right word at times, his enthusiasm more than compensates for his vocabulary deficiencies.

One evening, while addressing a parent-teacher group in Wisconsin, he referred to the town of "Feetsville," only to be interrupted by a pedant who said, "Mr. Logan, you're mistaken. It's Footsville, not Feetsville. You seem to have made a mistake."

"Sit down, teacher," grinned Johnny. "That ain't the last mistake you're gonna hear today."

BABY, IT'S COLD OUTSIDE

When Bob Buhl, the Milwaukee pitcher, visited the Mayo clinic to have his arm trouble diagnosed, the medicos couldn't pinpoint the source of pain. So they told Bob to return to Milwaukee and throw every day as hard as he could until the arm got as sore as he could stand it. Then return to the Clinic.

This ludicrous prescription recalls the story about the ball player who had a common cold. He went to the doctor who examined him and said, "Go home and take a hot bath. Then dry yourself off, go into your bedroom, open the window, and do toe-touching exercises for 15 minutes."

"But, Doc," protested the pitcher, "it's freezing outside. I'll catch pneumonia."

"Good," replied the doctor. "For that we have a cure."

UP IN THE AIR

Johnny Shives has a sharp sense of humor for an umpire. One of his reports to Carolina League president Bill Jessup carried this notation:

"Please take $5 of pitcher Red Willis's money. If you can find him an old resin bag, send it to him to practice throwing in the air."

LONG, LONG BRAILLE A-WINDING

Fresco Thompson had many a run-in with the umps in his days with the Dodgers, Giants and Phillies. One afternoon a question of the rules arose and the irate ump waved a rule book in Fresco's face. "I've got my rule book right here," he roared.

"How do you expect me to read it," snarled Fresco right back. "If it's yours, it must be written in Braille."

WHAT A RELIEF

The Giants made history in only one respect in 1957. They had an uncle-nephew combination on the pitching staff. On June 13, nephew Jim Davis held the Cubs for eight innings, then was bailed out of a tough spot by uncle Marv Grissom.

"At least," remarked a crestfallen Cub, "we made 'em holler uncle."

RIZZUTO BOO-BOOS

Phil Rizzuto, the ex-Yankee shortstopping great now helping Mel Allen with the radio and TV chores, is a thoroughly likable young fellow who's doing a warm, sincere job at the mike. But his inexperience manifests itself now and then in some amusing boo-boos.

When the disappointing Detroit Tigers came into town one p.m., Rizzuto announced that "soon as the Tigers get hitting, pitching, and fielding, they're going to be right up there in the race."

Watching the umpire dust off the plate: "There's Larry Napp dusting off home plate from Staten Island."

Anent Bob Cerv's broken jaw: "Bob's jaw is completely wired and he has difficulty with his breathing. The team trainer must room with him. For in his sleep the wire might gag him and he might choke to death—and that's dangerous!"

POP-UP DAZE

The one-time Minneapolis manager, Joe Cantillon, once used three pinch hitters in a single inning. All three popped up feebly. As they slumped back on the bench, Cantillon turned to the third failure and said with devastating softness: "You win, Gavvy. Yours was the highest."

BAD FOOTING

Back in the days of the Gashouse Gang, Tony Kaufmann, the St. Louis pitching coach, was trying to show a rookie how to stand on the rubber. But the smart-alecky youngster refused to listen.

The exasperated coach turned to a veteran observer nearby and asked, "Isn't his right foot in the wrong place, Mike?"

"Yeah," snapped the vet, "and so is his left. Both ought to be in Terre Haute."

FAREWELL TO ARMS

During a 16-inning affair with the Dodgers early in the 1957 season, the St. Louis Cardinals fielded an outfield consisting of Del Ennis, Chuck Harmon, and Wally Moon.

"Look at that Venus de Milo outfield," murmured a reporter in the press box. "Beautiful, but no arms."

A WALK IN THE SUN

Al Schacht, the "Clown Prince of Baseball," ran into an

old-timer who promptly began bragging about what a great hitter he had been: "My lifetime batting average was .390, and I wouldda hit .800 if them pitchers wasn't afraid to pitch to me."

As the two men reached a corner, the traffic light changed and the sign WALK lit up. "See," the old-timer chuckled, "they're still afraid to pitch to me!"

CALL OF THE WILD

A notorious bad-ball hitter, Yogi Berra went fishing for a terrible pitch very high and very outside, and struck out. A deep silence greeted him on his return to the dugout. Yogi waited vainly for a word from someone. Silence reigned supreme. Finally the irrepressible catcher blurted:

"How can a pitcher that wild stay in the league?"

TARS AND STRIPES

Yankee coach Charlie Keller had just entered the clubhouse when Yogi Berra strolled over. "Remember the first time you ever saw me, Charlie?" asked Yogi.

"Certainly," said Charlie. "You were just getting out of the Navy and were wearing a sailor suit."

"When you saw me in a sailor suit, I betcha never thought I looked like a ballplayer," grinned Berra.

"Looked like a ballplayer?" snapped the clubhouse man. "You didn't even look like a sailor!"

RASP-BERRA

Yogi Berra and Gil McDougald, waiting for a telecast, were watching a studio artist doodling. The fellow had drawn a picture of a stagecoach, without wheels.

"That's pretty good," remarked Gil. "But I don't see any wheels. What holds it up?"

"The bad guys," cracked Yogi.

IMPORTANCE OF BEING ERNEST

Yogi Berra finally caught up with Ernest Hemingway in Toots Shor's famous restaurant. The great novelist, bearded and wearing a battered hat and raincoat, was about to sally forth into the stormy night.

When Yogi returned to his table, he remarked to Tom Meany of the Yankee staff, "Gee! He's a character."

"He's a writer," said Meany.

"Yeah?" said Yogi, "with what paper?"

BOWLING ALONG

Yogi Berra recently opened a bowling alley and, as a get-acquainted stunt, gave away free the first two days' bowling. His affluent manager, Casey Stengel, chided him on his lack of business acumen.

"I'm a bank director in California," observed Stengel. "What do you think would happen if I opened my bank and let the customers help themselves for a couple of days?"

"It's not the same thing," snapped Berra. "Bowling balls are tougher to get past the guards than money."

TABLE SERVICE

The latest Yogi Berra yarn is relayed by Joe Garagiola, former big league catcher turned broadcaster and MC. Joe took Yogi to a well-known restaurant in New York, but couldn't be seated immediately. A long line of diners stood behind the rope waiting for a table.

Finally Berra turned to Garagiola and snorted, "No wonder nobody comes here. It's too crowded!"

ON LAND AND SEA

Yogi Berra was extolling the prowess of his teammate, Mickey Mantle. "Mantle," said Berra, "can hit just as good right-handed as he can left-handed. He's just naturally amphibious."

STRANGER THAN FICTION

Asked by a Florida scribe how he liked training in that state, Yogi pondered a moment, then replied, "I like it okay. The climate's good and you meet so many new strangers."

LEFT AT THE POST

Yogi Berra was explaining his after-dinner speaking difficulties to his friend, Jackie Farrell. "I'm always nervous at the start. But after a few words I'm okay."

"Well, Yogi," advised Farrell, "the mayor of the town is usually present and there's always the toastmaster. Why don't you get started by turning to the mayor on your right and saying, 'Mr. Mayor.' Then turn to the toastmaster on your left and say, 'Mr. Toastmaster.' That will get you started."

Berra pondered that one and then asked, "Yeah, but what happens if the mayor is on the left and the toastmaster on the right?"

MOTHER'S DAY

Early Wynn, the "old pro" of the White Sox pitching staff,

is a real hard-nosed competitor. At various functions he's invariably introduced as "a guy who wouldn't give his own mother a good pitch to hit."

Early now has a stock reply to that one. "Mother," he says, "was a helluva hitter."

STICK AROUND AWHILE

Sandy Koufax, the young Dodger left-hander, is one of the worst hitters ever to play the national pastime. One afternoon he took a mighty cut and, to everybody's astonishment, drove a triple to deep right center.

Perched on third, Sandy whispered to Coach Billy Herman, "Billy, I think I can steal home on this guy."

Herman groaned, "Sandy, it's taken you three years to get this far; hang around a while and enjoy it."

CADET CRUSHER

Every spring the Giants used to stop off at West Point for an exhibition game against the Cadets. During the reign of Leo Durocher, the Cadets used to love to ride him.

One afternoon a leather-lunged West Pointer roared, "Hey, Leo, how did a runt like you ever get into the big leagues?"

Durocher pinned back his ears with, "My congressman appointed me!"

I'VE GOT PLENTY OF NUTHIN

Good umpires always make it clear who's boss. In a close play at home one afternoon, Umpire Charlie Moran hesitated on the call. The catcher barked, "Well, is he safe or out?"

"Son," remarked Charlie softly, "Till I call it, it ain't nuthin'."

QUATRAIN CHECK

In winter when it's cold out,
Appears the baseball holdout.
In spring when it's warm out
He gets his uniform out.

HE MADE A HIT

When the Pirates' great second baseman, Bill Mazeroski, came up to the majors, he immediately proved he was a great glove man but gave little indication of any prowess with the bat. One of his rabid boosters told a Pittsburgh scribe what a credit Bill was to the game.

"He's clean-cut, clean-living, and church-going," enthused the friend. "A fine boy, a model for teen-agers."

The sportswriter listened politely, then remarked: "Very nice, but the Pirates would be better off right now with a juvenile delinquent who can hit."

UPPER BIRTH

The Yankees didn't endear themselves to the good Milwaukee people in the 1957 World Series, and one of the local sportswriters wanted to make sure he wasn't mistaken for a New Yorker. Getting off a bus at County Stadium, he loudly declared, "I want everybody to know that I'm not a New Yorker."

This made the *New York Times* diamond expert, John Drebinger, kind of indignant, and he snapped, "Well, I'm proud of being a New Yorker. In fact, I was born on the sidewalks of New York!"

"How uncomfortable," murmured the other.

INTERNATIONAL ANTHEM

An Irishman named O'Shea came to America and wanted

to attend a big league game. Since all the seats were sold out, the management set him up on the flagpole. When he returned to Ireland, his neighbors asked him: "What kind of people are the Americans?"

"Great," he said. "They gave me a special seat and just before the game started, they all stood up and sang, 'O'Shea can you see?' "

GNAT FOR PUBLICATION

In his first time at bat in the majors, Johnny Temple took a called third strike. He whirled around and cussed out the ump, Larry Goetz. The veteran arbiter promptly tossed him out of the game.

"Why do you let the other ball players object and not me?" demanded the hot-blooded Cincinnati rookie.

"I don't mind when the lions and tigers get on me," replied Goetz. "But when the nits and gnats do it, it's too much."

TWIN PUN-ISHMENT

Bobby Bragan, the former big league pilot, enjoys a good pun. When he was managing Pittsburgh, he traded Dale Long to the Cubs for Dee Fondy. He announced it in this fashion: "The absence of Long will make Pittsburgh hearts grow Fondy."

A nearby sportswriter, thinking of Cincinnati's fine trade with the Cubs for Don Hoak, remarked, "And the little acorn at third base has grown into a mighty Hoak."

RETARDED CAREER

Coming up for his first turn at bat as a major leaguer, the

rookie looked at Umpire Bill McGowan and did a double take. "I hope you're a better ump up here than you were in the minors a couple of years ago," he blurted.

McGowan doffed his mask and said softly, "Young man, your major league debut has just been delayed by at least one day. Scram!"

O FOR FOUR

The Cardinals, preparing for their trip to Japan in the fall of 1958, were being given their overseas "shots" by the team doctor. Ken Boyer, investigating the sera, came across one marked "cholera."

"What's that for?" he asked.

"When you get the 'collar' in four," replied Stan Musial, "that's cholera."

UNDERPRIVILEGED WORKER

In one of those lazy spring exhibition games, Clem Labine was murdered by the Yankees. "What happened?" queried a scribe. "Were you wild or was it that you just didn't have your stuff?"

"I got hit," the great Dodger pitcher snapped. "What do you expect for $25 a week?"

SPEECHLESS MICKEY

Though Mickey Mantle has been around for nine years, he's still inarticulate and runs like a thief from after-dinner speaking chores. But he is not without a sense of humor. At a big blow-out in St. Petersburg, Larry McQueen, the toastmaster, announced there would be no speeches. Then in the next breath he called upon Mantle for a few words.

Mickey brought his bat around fast. "When Mr. McQueen said there would be no speeches," he said, "I tore mine up."

RED, RED ROBIN

One of Robin Roberts' most notable feats was fanning three Pirates in a row after being hit for a triple. He whiffed Castiglione on five pitches, Kiner on four, and Joe Garagiola on just three. This made Garagiola spittin' mad.

"It's darn embarrassing," fumed Joe. "He should have at least worked on me a little."

STAN FAST

One afternoon the Cubs started a rookie pitcher against the Cardinals. When Stan Musial came to bat, Joe Garagiola signed for a slider. The rookie shook him off. Next Garagiola ordered a curve. Again the rookie shook him off. Then the catcher signalled for a fast ball. Still the shake-off. So Garagiola called for time and went out to the mound.

"Just what do you want to throw?" he snapped.

"Nothing," replied the pitcher. "I just want to hold on to the ball."

"Don't be afraid of Musial," soothed the catcher. "Do you think I am?"

"No," answered the pitcher, "but you don't have to play in front of him."

COAT SHORT

It was a boiling hot day in St. Louis and Umpire Red Ormsby shed his coat. In about the fifth inning, Jimmy Dykes slyly called out, "Hey, Red, don't you miss your coat?"

"No," answered Red, "why should I?"

"Because," snapped Dykes, "you've been missing every-thing else all afternoon!"

BACK-FIRE

The spectacular "Salute to Baseball" was running along beautifully over the nation's TV screens when emcee Art Linkletter asked 12-year-old Carl Fields which sport he liked best.

"Basketball," the kid answered brightly.

NO BOTHER AT ALL

Asked whether it bothered him to be compared with Duke Snider all the time, Willie Mays snorted, "Bother me? Why, I'm happy about it. Some fellows play for 20 years without being compared to anybody."

HEY THERE, TOMMY MANVILLE!

With the opening day of the baseball season just 24 hours away, the office boy applied for a day off.

"What is it this time?" snapped the office manager. "You've asked time off for your grandfather's funeral four times already."

"Today," replied the boy, "my grandmother's getting married again."

TABACCHI ROAD

When umpire Frank Tabacchi came into the American League, Senor Al Lopez, Cleveland manager, was warned not to call him any Spanish names. "This fellow spent 10 years in Latin American countries and also studied Span-ish," Lopez was told.

"So what?" Lopez snorted. "I always tell off the umps in English. It's more fun when they understand."

PIRATE GOLD

The spirit of the rejuvenated Pittsburgh Pirates was best exemplified by Eddie O'Brien. Rarely did Eddie get into a ball game. But when he did, it was usually as a pinch runner. But Eddie never permitted this to get him down.

Early in the 1957 season, Manager Bobby Bragan sent him in to run for Dick Cole. Eventually he scored a crucial run and in the dressing room he strutted around proud as a pouter pigeon.

"I finally made the grade," he grinned. "Now I know that outside of Wes Santee I'm the only professional runner in the country."

LONG LOSSES

Back in the days when Casey Stengel was managing the dreadful Braves, the Boston park was a huge prairie where the pitchers threw down the middle, the batters hit fly balls, and the Braves usually lost in an hour and a half or less. So Casey called a meeting.

"Now, boys," he said, "I know you're doing the best you can, and I'm not complaining about losing. But, gee, couldn't you take a little longer doing it?"

24 HOUR RECALL

Many old-timers insist that Josh Gibson, the old Negro catcher, was the greatest backstop of all time. And they could very well be right. One thing is sure: he could hit a ball out of sight.

One hazy afternoon, he hit a towering fly in the Pittsburgh ballpark. The umpire waited a long while for the ball to come down. When it didn't, he had to rule it a home run.

In Philadelphia next day, Gibson stepped into the batter's box when a ball suddenly zoomed out of space and was caught by the center fielder.

"Yer out!" shouted the ump. "I mean yesterday in Pitts-burgh!"

HITLESS WONDERS

The day after Don Larsen no-hit no-walked them, the Brooklyn Dodgers straggled onto the field to take their licks in the batting cage. Don Zimmer was among the first on the field and noticed that the bats hadn't yet been brought out.

"Hell," yelled Zimmer. "What do we use to hit?"

"Try the same things you used yesterday!" hollered Joe Becker, the Dodger pitching coach.

THE BIG BITE

Roy Campanella would just as soon forget the 1956 season. All the pitchers took turns at fooling him, and Campy wound up with a .215 batting average.

Flying home from the last critical series with the Pirates, the Dodgers were discussing fishing. Carl Furillo proudly displayed a delicately made trout fly. He handed it to Pee Wee Reese who extended it to Campy. But Roy refused to take it.

"Put it away," he snapped with feigned anger.

"What's the matter with it?" asked Furillo.

"I've been biting at everything," the catcher said, "and I'm liable to take a bite at that, too!"

$64,000 *QUESTION*

Dee Williams, former Cub catcher, silently watched one of his teammates jawing away at Umpire Charlie Berry. Naturally the player lost the argument and everybody started moving back to their positions. It was then that Dee turned to Berry:

"Charlie," he said quietly, "answer me one question: How do you get your square head in that round mask?"

JUMPING AT CONCUSSIONS

After being severely beaned, Don Zimmer was visited in the hospital by Walt Alston. The Dodger manager tried to cheer up the injured shortstop by telling him that he'd be back in the game in a couple of weeks.

"I wouldn't say that," grinned Pee Wee Reese's understudy. "I've been out longer than that even when I wasn't hurt."

LONE RANGER

Experts believe that if Vinegar Bend Mizell could perfect a change of pace to go with his fast ball, there'd be no other left-handed pitcher in the majors like him.

Lefty Gomez used to hear the same thing from Joe McCarthy. "He spent 10 years trying to teach me a change of pace," says Lefty, "and at the end of my career that's all I had left—and there was no other pitcher like me."

SATCHEL PRAISE

In Babe Ruth's first year with the Yankees, he drew Ping Bodie for a roommate. But they were roomies in name only. The Babe was such a confirmed playboy that Bodie saw little of him. Someone once asked Ping, "Who are you rooming with?"

"Babe Ruth's valises," he replied.

WAITING FOR THE MAIL

Earl Combs came up to the Yankees with a great reputation as a base stealer. "So you're pretty fast, eh?" Manager Miller Huggins asked.

"Yes, sir," replied Combs. "They used to call me the mail-carrier down in Louisville."

"Well, up here they'll just call you the waiter," smiled Hug. "We've got a couple of guys called Babe Ruth and Bob Meusel, and if you get on base, you just wait till they knock you in."

FANNING BEE

Watching Herb Score strike out 13 Orioles and allow just one hit, the nice old lady seeing her first game was totally unimpressed. Leaving the park her only comment was:

"It's a good thing the Orioles got that hit. Otherwise we wouldn't have seen ANYTHING!"

APRIL SHOWERS

An old pitcher persuaded Rip Collins, the great ex-big league slugger, to come out and make a talk at a local banquet. En route to the hall, the pitcher implored Rip not to make him look bad before the home folks. "They think I was a great pitcher and I wish you wouldn't do anything to spoil their illusion." Naturally, Rip agreed.

So the pitcher got up and introduced Rip in this fashion: "I want you to meet Rip Collins, one of the greatest hitters that ever came up to the big leagues. But he never got a hit off me in his life."

Though stunned for a moment, Rip still got his bat around in time. "That's absolutely true," he remarked, after getting to his feet. "You see, I used to bat fifth and by the time I came up, our friend here was already in the shower."

MIND OVER MATTER

Don Newcombe is one of those pitchers who's always complaining about something—real or fancied. During one spell under Manager Burt Shotton, he kept insisting that his arm hurt.

"It's all in your imagination," Shotton grunted.

A day or two later, Shotton told Newcombe to start warming up. Big Newk took a couple of pitches and winced with pain.

"My imagination is hurting again," he told Burt.

PIN-POINTING

When Jack Tighe was managing the Flint club, the league prexy was Tom Halligan, a bowling alley tycoon. Tighe once became embroiled with one of the umpires, and blew his stack.

"Mister," he snapped, "I know you're working for the president of this league. But he's got you in the wrong job. You should be looking at a different kind of strike . . . and setting up pins for him!"

JOLLEY WELL-SAID

The fabulous Smead Jolley may not have been much of a fielder, but he certainly could hit. At that, he didn't know anything about the science of hitting. He just swatted the ball by instinct.

A rookie once approached him and asked, "When I hit, Mr. Jolley, should I place the left foot closer to the plate or is it better to keep both feet even?"

Smead scratched his head. "Look, kid, when you go to the plate, never be superstitious."

LONG STRETCH

As a rookie with the Yankees, Lefty Gomez once took a full wind-up with a man on first. The runner promptly stole second, and Manager Joe McCarthy went out to the mound and cautioned Lefty to watch himself. Gomez wound up again, and the runner stole third. Again the conference, again the windup, and again the steal—this time of home with the winning run.

"That was the longest wind-up in history," Gomez now confesses. "I wound up in St. Paul."

SOMETHIN' FOR NOTHIN'

How good is this Hank Aaron? Tremendous, says his manager, Fred Haney. "I once gave him the hit sign with 3 and 0 and he took the pitch right down the middle. On the next pitch he walked, and I met him at first base.

" 'Henry,' I said, 'what was the matter with that 3-0 pitch?'

"Henry answered, 'Well, he just took a little bit off it, and when I'm hittin' 3 and 0 I want somethin' on it, not off it.' "

CRAZY, MAN!

Jocko Munch, the famous minor league catcher, was in

a terrible batting slump when his club booked an exhibition game with a nearby insane asylum. In one of the early innings, one of the inmates jumped out of the stands, set up near the first-base line, made nine imaginary pitches, and returned to his seat. The fellow repeated his performance for three straight innings.

Jocko turned to one of the attendants and asked, "What's the guy think he's doing?"

The attendant explained, "He imagines he's a pitcher who's pitching a no-hit game."

"If I don't get a hit in this game," replied Jocko, "he'll have a catcher tomorrow."

COMING THROUGH THE WHEAT

Subtle was just the word for the way Connie Mack used to handle his 1929-31 championship Philadelphia Athletics. One day Max Bishop was tossed out at third on what should have been an easy three-bagger. Next morning at breakfast, Mr. Mack discovered his star second baseman sitting in front of a huge stack of wheat cakes.

"Max," he said apologetically, "if you hit another triple today, I'd suggest that you stop at third base."

CAN'T FIND THE HANDLE

With two out and a runner on second in the 12th, Don Hoak of the Cubs nubbed one down the first-base line. Gil Hodges swooped down, but the ball hit the bag and spun toward second. Hodges stabbed for it, but the ball twisted away. He stabbed again and again. Then Jackie Robinson horned in. The Dodger pair began flailing away like tenderfeet trying to nail a squirming rattler with canoe paddles.

Finally, Hodges looked up. Hoak was safe at first and the winning run was crossing the plate.

"Hit it again, Jackie," he wryly remarked. "It's still breathing."

DOUBLE-TALK

Wanna know the secret of Mickey Mantle's success? Big muscles? Nah. Great timing? Nope. Speed? Uh-uh. It was his extrapyramidal influences. Oh heck, let *Scope*, the medical news weekly, explain it to you:

"Mantle observes the ball is thrown with binocular series of images reflected on the occipital cortex; information is relayed to the frontal association areas where future trajectory of ball is predicted. In motor cortex, the necessary neurons are fired and muscular action results. Motor impulses are superimposed on extrapyramidal influences from the cerebellum, basal ganglia, etc."

CUT-RATE BASEBALL

The Indianapolis Indians of the American Association are municipally owned by 6,672 fans. Thus, when a visiting batter once fouled ball after ball into the stands (at $2.75 each), a spectator-stockholder yelled:

"Hey, let's walk this guy. It's much cheaper!"

MITCHELL FIELD DAY

For day-in and day-out humorous sports-commentating,

you'd have to go a long way to find the peer of Jerry Mitchell, of the *New York Post*. Following is the kind of bright, witty writing that he bats out every day:

- **Ladies of fashion** aren't the only citizens who got the sack this season. The baseball season isn't half over and two managers are already wearing dismissal duds.
- **Detroit fired** Jack Tighe a few weeks ago and Cleveland canned Bobby Bragan last week. In a number of other towns, managers go to bed nights wondering what the morning will bring and whether it would be a bad idea to get up to find out.
- **These are also worry weeks** for such as Walter Alston and Mayo Smith. Every approaching footstep may be that of the general manager wearing bunions that bounce.
- **Club officials** have said that Charley Dressen won't get the manager's job again if Alston gets the heave-o, but we wouldn't bet the family jewels on that, even if they are from a fire sale at the five and dime.
- **The only statement** by the Dodgers' front-office that we'd bank on would be a flat, forthright announcement that the sun sinks in the West.
- **And even then** we'd have a suspicion that Walter O'Malley might manage to move it if the price were right.
- **Cleveland has become** a tougher place to manage a club than Havana during an uprising. They didn't invent the razzberry there, but they sure wired it for sound.
- **Years ago they chased** the Indian Love Call out of town as a lunatic's lullaby. The only tune they like is the squeak as a manager gets the gate.
- **In baseball circles** the Cleveland bench has become known as the hottest seat outside of the electric job in the big house.
- **The two most popular questions** in Cleveland every summer are: (a) When are they gonna do something about that smell off the lake front? And (b) who's the next manager of the Indians?
- **As a player,** Joe Gordon was one of the most relaxed citizens not living in Milltown, but he'll need all the casualness at his command to work under Frank Lane. The man's harder to please than the fellow grading examination papers at a school for counterfeiters.

THE CLICHE EXPERT TESTIFIES ON BASEBALL*

By Frank Sullivan

Art by H. a. s.

Mighty batsman

Q—Mr. Arbuthnot, you state that your grandmother has died and you'd like the afternoon off to go to her funeral.

A—That is correct.

Q—You are an expert in the clichés of baseball—right?

A—I pride myself on being well versed in the stereotypes of our national pastime.

Q—Well, we'll test you. Who plays baseball?

A—Big-league baseball is customarily played by brilliant out-fielders, veteran hurlers, powerful sluggers, towering first base-men, key moundsmen, fleet base runners, ace southpaws, scrappy little shortstops, ex-college stars, relief artists, rifle-armed twirl-ers, dependable mainstays, doughty righthanders, streamlined backstops, redoubtable infielders, erstwhile Dodgers, veteran sparkplugs, sterling moundsmen, aging twirlers, and rookie sensations.

Reprinted by permission. © 1949 The New Yorker Magazine Inc.

ROOKIE SENSATION

Q—What other names are rookie sensations known by?

A—They are also known as aspiring rookies, sensational new-comers, promising freshmen, highly touted striplings, and youngsters who will bear watching.

Q—What's the manager of a baseball team called?

A—A veteran pilot. Or youthful pilot. But he doesn't manage the team.

Q—No? What does he do?

A—He guides its destinies.

Q—How?

A—By the use of managerial strategy.

Q—Mr. Arbuthnot, please describe the average major-league-baseball athlete?

A—Well, he comes in three sizes, or types. The first type is tall, slim, lean, towering, rangy, husky, big, strapping, sturdy, powerful, lanky, rawboned, and rugged.

Q—Quite a hunk of athlete.

A—Well, those are the adjectives usage required for the description of the Type One, or Ted Williams, ballplayer.

Q—What is Type Two like?

A—He is chunky or stocky—that is to say, Yogi Berra.

Q—And the third?

A—The third type is elongated and does not walk. He is Ol' Satchmo, Satchel Paige.

Q—What do you mean Satchmo doesn't walk?

A—Not in the sports pages, he doesn't. He ambles.

Q—You mentioned a hurler. What is a hurler?

A—A hurler is a twirler.

Q—Well, what is a twirler?

A—A twirler is a flinger, a tosser. He's a moundsman. He officiates on the mound. When the veteran pilot tells a hurler he is to twirl on a given day, that is a mound assignment, and the hurler who has been told to twirl is the mound nominee for that game.

Q—You mean he pitches? What's the pitcher for the other team called?

A—He is the mound adversary, or mound opponent, of the mound nominee. That makes them rival hurlers, or twirlers. They face each other and have a mound duel.

Q—Who wins?

A—The mound victor wins, and as a result he is a mound ace, or ace moundsman.

Q—I see. Why does the losing moundsman lose?

A—Because he issues, grants, yields, allows, or permits too many hits or walks, or both.

FLEET BASE-RUNNER

Q—A bit on the freehanded side, eh? Where does the mound victor go if he pitches the entire game?

A—He goes all the way.

Q—And how does the mound adversary who has been knocked out of the box explain his being driven off the mound?

A—He says, *"I had trouble with my control,"* or *"My curve wasn't working,"* or *"I just didn't have anything today."*

Q—What happens if a mound ace issues, grants, yields, allows, or permits too many hits and walks?

A—In that case, sooner or later, rumors are rife. Either that or they are rampant.

Q—Rife where?

A—In the front office.

Q—What's that?

A—That's the place where baseball's biggies—also known as baseball moguls—do their asking.

Q—What do they ask for?

A—Waivers on erratic southpaws.

Q—What do baseball biggies do when they are not asking for waivers?

A—They count the gate receipts, buy promising rookies, sell aging twirlers, and stand loyally by the manager.

Q—And what does the manager do?

A—He guides the destinies of the team and precipitates arguments with the men in blue.

Q—What men in blue?

A—The umpires, or arbiters.

Q—What kind of arguments does the manager precipitate?

A—Heated arguments.

Q—And the men in blue do what to him and other players who precipitate heated arguments?

A—They send, relegate, banish, or thumb them to the showers.

Q—Mr. Arbuthnot, how do you, as a cliche expert, refer to first base?

A—First base is the initial sack.

Q—And second base?

A—The keystone sack.

Q—What's third base called?

A—The hot corner. The first inning is the initial frame, and an inning without runs is a scoreless stanza.

Q—And what's a bat?

A—The bat is the willow, or the wagon tongue, or the piece of lumber. In the hands of a mighty batsman, it is the mighty bludgeon.

Q—What does a mighty batsman do?

A—He amasses runs. He connects with the old apple. He belts 'em and he clouts 'em.

Q—Clouts what?

A—Circuit clouts.

Q—What are they?

A—Home runs. Know what the mighty batsman does to the mighty bludgeon?

Q—No. What?

A—He wields it. Know what kind of orgies he fancies?

Q—What kind?

A—Batting orgies. Slugfests. That's why his team pins.

Q—Pins what?

A—All its hopes on him.

Q—And how many kinds of baseball games are there?

A—Five main classifications: scheduled tussles, crucial contests, pivotal games, drab frays, and arclight tussles.

Q—And what does the team that wins—

A—Sir, a baseball team never wins. It scores a victory, or gains one, or chalks one up. Or it snatches.

Q—Snatches what?

A—Victory from the jaws of defeat.

Q—I see. Well, what do the teams that chalk up victories do to the teams that lose?

A—They nip, top, wallop, trounce, rout, subdue, smash, drub, paste, trip, crush, whitewash, bop, check, hammer, pop, wham, clout, and blank the visitors. Or they zero them.

Q—Gracious sakes!

A—Oh, that isn't the half of it. They do other things to the visitors.

Q—Is it possible?

A—Certainly. They jolt them, or deal them a jolt. They also halt, thump, vanquish, flatten, scalp, blast, mow down, topple, pound, rap, sink, baffle, thwart, foil, and nick.

Q—Do the losers do anything at all to the victors?

A—Yes. They bow to the victors. And they taste.

Q—Taste what?

A—Defeat. They trail. They take a drubbing, pasting, or shellacking.

Q—What about the victors?

A—They loom as flag contenders.

Q—Mr. Arbuthnot, what is the first sign of spring?

A—Well, a robin, of course.

Q—Yes, but I'm thinking of our subject here. How about when the ballplayers go south for spring training?

A—Ballplayers don't go south for spring training.

Q—Why, they do!

A—They do *not*. They wend their way southward.

Q—Oh, I see. Well, do all ballplayers wend their way southward?

A—No. One remains at home.

Q—Who is he?

A—The lone holdout.

VETERAN PILOT

Q—Why does the lone holdout remain at home?
A—He refuses to ink pact.
Q—What do you mean by that?
A—He won't affix his Hancock to his contract.
Q—From whom?
A—From baseball's biggies.
Q—And what do baseball's biggies do to the lone holdout?
A—They attempt to lure him back into the fold.

RIFLE-ARMED TWIRLER

Q—How?
A—By offering him new contract.

Q—What does lone holdout do then?

A—He weighs offer. If he doesn't like it, he balks at terms. If he does like it, he inks pact and gets pay hike.

Q—How much pay hike?

A—An undisclosed amount in excess of.

Q—That makes him what?

A—One of the highest-paid baseball stars in the annals of the game, barring Ruth.

Q—What if baseball's biggies won't give lone holdout pay hike?

A—In that case, lone holdout takes pay cut, old salary, or job in filling station in home town.

Q—Now, when baseball players reach the spring training camp and put on their uniforms—

A—May I correct you again, sir? Baseball players do not put on uniforms. They don them.

Q—I see. What for?

A—For a practice session or strenuous workout.

Q—And why must they have a strenuous workout?

A—Because they must shed the winter's accumulation of excess avoirdupois.

Q—You mean they must lose weight?

A—You put it in a nutshell. They must be streamlined, so they plunge.

Q—Plunge into what?

A—Into serious training.

Q—Can't get into serious training except by plunging, eh?

A—No. Protocol requires that they plunge. Training season gets under way in Grapefruit and Citrus Leagues. Casey Stengel bars night life.

Q—Mr. Arbuthnot, what is the opening game of the season called?

A—Let me see-e-e. It's on the tip of my tongue. Isn't that aggravating? Ah, I have it—the opener! At the opener, fifty-two thousand two hundred and ninety-three fans watch Giants bow to Dodgers.

Q—And how do they get into the ballpark?

A—They click through the turnstiles.

Q—Now then, Mr. Arbuthnot, the climax of the baseball season is the World Series, is it not?

A—That's right.

Q—And what is the World Series called?

A—It's the fall classic, or crucial contest, also known as the fray, the epic struggle, and the Homeric struggle. It is part of the American scene, like ham and eggs or pumpkin pie. It's a colorful event.

Q—What is it packed with?

A—Thrills. Drama.

Q—What kind of drama?

A—Sheer or tense.

Q—Why does it have to be packed with thrills and drama?

A—Because if it isn't, it becomes drab fray.

Q—And the city in which the fall classic is held is what?

A—The city is baseball mad.

Q—And the hotels?

A—The hotels are jammed. Rooms are at a premium.

Q—Tickets, also, I presume.

A—Tickets? If you mean the cards of admission to the fall classic, they are referred to as elusive Series ducats, and they *are* at a premium, though I would prefer to say that they are scarcer than the proverbial hen's teeth.

Q—What does the great outpouring of fans do?

A—It storms the portals and, of course, clicks through the turnstiles.

Q—Causing what?

A—Causing attendance records to go by the board. Stands fill early. The crowd yells itself hoarse.

Q—What else does the crowd do?

A—Its pent-up emotions are released. It rides the men in blue.

Q—What makes a baseball biggie unhappy on the morning of a Series tussle?

A—Leaden skies.

Q—Who is to blame for leaden skies?

A—A character known to the scribes as Jupiter Pluvius, or Jupe.

Q—What does rain dampen?

A—The ardor of the fans.

Q—If the weather clears, who gets credit for that?

A—Another character, known as Old Sol.

Q—Now, the team that wins the Series—

A—Again, I'm sorry to correct you, sir. A team does not win a Series. It wraps it up. It clinches it.

Q—Well, then what?

A—Then the newly crowned champions repair to their locker room.

Q—What reigns in the locker room?

A—Pandemonium, bedlam, and joy.

Q—In the locker room of the losers, what is as thick as a day in—I mean so thick you could cut it with a knife?

A—Gloom. The losers are devoid.

Q—Devoid of what?

A—Animation.

Q—Why?

A—Because they came apart at the seams in the pivotal tussle.

Q—What happens to the newly crowned champions later?

A—They are hailed, acclaimed and fêted. They receive mighty ovations and boisterous demonstrations.

Q—And when those are over?

A—They split the Series purse and go hunting.

Q—Mr. Arbuthnot, if a powerful slugger or mighty batsman wields a mighty bludgeon to such effect that he piles up a record number of circuit clouts, what does that make him?

A—That is very apt to make him most valuable player of the year.

Q—And that?

A—That makes the kids of America look up to him as their hero.

Q—If most valuable player of the year continues the batting orgies that make the kids of America worship him, what then?

A—Then he becomes one of Baseball's Immortals. He is enshrined in Baseball's Hall of Fame.

Q—And after that?

A—Someday he retires and becomes veteran scout, or veteran coach, or veteran pilot. Or sports broadcaster.

Q—Thank you, Mr. Arbuthnot. You have been most helpful. I won't detain you any longer, and I hope your grandmother's funeral this afternoon is a tense drama packed with thrills. Thanks a lot. Goodbye now.

A—Thanks a lot. Goodbye now.

Q—Hold on a moment, Mr. Arbuthnot. Just for my own

LOSING MOUNDSMAN

curiosity—couldn't you have said "thanks" and "goodbye" and let it go at that, without adding that "lot" and "now" malarkey?

A—I could have, but it would have cost me my title as a cliche expert.

AROUND THE WHIRL IN 180 DAZE

March 1: Old Phil Greybeard, 48-year-old dean of the Philadelphia Mares' pitching staff, appeared fit and trim as he entrained for the Mares' spring camp in Muddywater, Fla. "At 245 pounds I may be a little heavy," he admitted. "But I've got it evenly distributed over my frame." The 5'3" righthander expects to win 20 games this year. "And if I don't win 20, you can bet your spikes I'll improve on my 1957 record," he declared. Old Phil had a big year last season, winning 3 and losing 14—his best mark since 1936.

March 5: Old Phil Greybeard tried his first half-speed curve today, and is now resting comfortably in the camp infirmary.

Trainer Frank Whycheck is hopeful of a quick recovery. "The shoulder bone is still attached to the arm bone," he assured the Mares' manager, Mayo Clinick.

March 8: The Dean of the Mares' staff, Old Phil Greybeard, continues to amaze camp observers with his condition and strong throwing. He went one full inning in the first Yannigan-Regular practice game, and was hit for only two cheap triples.

March 12: With the Mares ready to start their spring exhibition series, Old Phil Greybeard appears to be the "meal ticket" of old. "My back hasn't kicked up since last December, when I had my spine removed," he alleges. "And those bone chips in my head no longer interfere with my pitching motion. Did that line drive in the first inning hurt my leg? Not a bit. Just splintered the knee cap. That's all."

March 17: Old Phil Greybeard started against the Pittsburgh Lawmen yesterday and retired all three men he was called upon to face! Donald caught the first hitter's pop-up against

the monument 575 feet from the plate. Ferucci then speared
the second batter's soft liner just as it was about to clear the
40-foot fence in left center, and then Old Phil bore down and
got the third man out trying to stretch a triple into a homer.

April 1: After three consecutive innings of scoreless pitching
this spring, Old Phil Greybeard has been temporarily sidelined
with a mild case of senility. "Nothing to it," he sniffed. "I had
it in '28 and it only laid me up for six months."

April 14: Manager Mayo Clinick announced that Old Phil
Greybeard will definitely start the second game of Sunday's
double-header against the St. Louis Bishops. "The old soupbone is at fit as it'll ever be," declares Old Phil, "and I'll check-
mate every one of them Bishops." When queried about this
sudden burst of metaphor, Greybeard confessed he has turned
serious and is now reading the autobiography of Yogi Berra.

April 18: Old Phil Greybeard made his first start of the season and came through with a tremendous effort—setting an all-
time mark for extra base hits allowed in two-thirds of an inning.
Upon being removed with six runs in and the bases clogged,
Old Phil announced that the cold weather has bothered him.
"Wait till July," he vowed. "The old soupbone needs that hot
sun."

May 2: With the Mares hopelessly trailing the San Francisco
Midgets, 17-3, Old Phil Greybeard was brought in to mop up
in the last two innings. He yielded three runs in the eighth on
seven consecutive singles, then shut the door on the Midgets

with the aid of an unassisted triple play. The Mares, inspired
by this sensational relief stunt, went on to establish a new record
by clobbering eight Midget pitchers for 17 hits and 22 runs.
Greybeard then set the Midgets down in the ninth with nothing
more damaging than two home runs, and ambled off the field
with his first victory of the season. "I'm going to demand a

starting assignment," gurgled the happy victor while taking his hormone shots in the locker room.

June 27: The Mares sank into fourth place last night, when the Milwaukee Cravens drove Old Phil Greybeard to cover with a 10-run barrage in one and a third innings. Old Phil blamed the evening dew for his downfall. "But I'm not alibi-ing," he added.

July 22: In one of his infrequent mound appearances, Old Phil Greybeard nearly lasted an entire inning yesterday against the Los Angeles Codgers. He got two men out smoothly enough —one man for batting out of turn and the other for failing to touch third base on an inside-the-park homer—then the Codgers batted around three times. "It's those bone chips in my head," Greybeard explained under the showers. "They locked up my arm. But I'm not alibiing."

August 5: Old Phil Greybeard caused a sensation against the Chicago Cups in a twi-night twin bill by walking a total of 14 batters in one and two-thirds innings. "Nothing to worry about," Greybeard assured his stricken manager. "It was that sticky summer heat. Wait till the cool weather sets in in September."

September 18: It was "Old Phil Night" at Mares' Park yesterday, and the Section 8 Marching and Chowder Society heaped at least $45,000 worth of gifts upon their beloved old mediocrity. In a remarkable sporting gesture, every club in the League sent Old Phil a telegram reading: "Wish you'll be around forever, Phil." The Mares organization will perpetuate Greybeard's memory by erecting a monument on the spot where he has served so long and faithfully—under the showers.

October 1: Old Phil Greybeard, after 28 years of service to the Philadelphia Mares—interrupted by two world wars and the Battle of the Alamo—has finally called it a day. In announcing his retirement, Old Phil declared that baseball is no longer fun at his age and he wanted to spend more time with his growing youngsters. "I've been away from home so long," he says, "that my younger boy has difficulty recognizing me—and he's 27 years old."

January 17: Interrupted in his favorite position—standing under the showers—Old Phil Greybeard coyly alleged that he hadn't said "positively" when he announced his retirement back on October 1. Informed of this sensational development, Manager Mayo Clinick entrained immediately for Milltown.

March 1: Old Phil Greybeard, 49-year-old dean of the Philadelphia Mares' pitchers, appeared fit and trim as he entrained for the Mares' spring camp at Muddywater, Fla. "I expect to win 20 games this year," he announced. "And if I don't win 20, you can bet your spikes I'll improve on my 1958 record." Old Phil had a big year last season, winning 2 and losing 17— for his second best year since 1936.

IMPERFECT DIAMONDS

Single—the sublime state for which every married man yearns.
Triple Play—a lightninglike sequence of events after losing your big game wherein your children hiss you, your community ostracizes you, and your school fires you.

Home Run—when the little woman, after taking your guff all season, packs up and runs to mother.

Sacrifice—the sanity you have to give up to go into coaching.

Fadeaway—what old soldiers who never die, do slowly.

Hook Slide—a trombone that's seen better days.

Left Field—Moscow, Russia.

Texas Leaguer—the kind of hit which fills coaches' lunatic asylums.

Double Steal—when your wallet and watch are lifted at the same time.

First Base—what you never can get to on your first date with a virtuous maiden.

Foul line—the patois of the bleacherites.

Curve—what every principal throws when you ask for a raise.

Choke-Up—what every self-respecting coach does upon receiving a raise.

Screwball—the sportswriter who predicts you'll have a winning season.

Grounders—smog, lightning, and fog to the air lines.

Rubber—a trainer, a game of bridge, a pencil end, or a coach who believes in rabbit's feet.

Batter's Box—where the little woman stores her dough.

Clean-Up Man—the fellow who comes around once a week to restore order in the household.

Lead-Off Man—first tenor in a choir.

Extra Base—a fellow who beats his wife is this.

Stretch Motion—what sportswriters wait for publicity men to do when the dinner bill comes around.

Suicide Squeeze—demanding a raise after a losing season.

Hit-and-Run—what to do against a big guy who picks on you.

Umpire—an arrogant blind man who persecutes clean-cut American boys.

Fat Pitch—the corned beef in a cheap delicatessen.

Brush Him Back—how to handle a jaywalker who crosses in front of you.

Wasted Pitch—what your line amounts to when the girl says no.

Clutch Hitter—remember Joey Maxim?

Cut-Off—favorite tactic of the woman driver.

Pitcher—an object with long ears holding large quantities of beverages, often mistaken for a coach.

Seventh Inning Stretch—girdle-adjustment time on Ladies' Day.

Grass Cutter—the instrument Junior can never find whenever the lawn needs trimming.

One-Hand Stab—the life-saving grab at a strap in the subway rush hour.

Line Drive—Sis's annual plea for a telephone of her own.

Crouch Stance—the position assumed by coaches whenever the sports scribes start hurling brick-bats.

Pop Fly—a ridiculous piece of fishing gear with which Dad is remembered on Father's Day.

Pick-Up—major activity of sailors on shore leave.

Deliberate Walk—whenever the kids start yowling and the little woman starts nagging, hubby takes one of these.

Sign Stealer—a juvenile delinquent who collects traffic and park stanchions.

Knuckle Ball—a picnic for the pig gourmet.

Shortstop—jamming on the brakes when the light suddenly turns red.

Bunt—what every red-blooded American slugger always messes up when you ask him to do it.

HOW THE MIGHTY SWAT MULLIGAN FOILED THE TWO-HANDED CURVER

By BOZEMAN BULGER

(Back in the Golden Age of Sports Bozeman Bulger's column in the New York World *was "must" reading for baseball fans. One of the greatest sports humorists of the time he created a character, "Swat Mulligan," who ranks with the best in baseball whimsy. The writer's favorite Swat Mulligan saga follows.)*

Bobbletown, June 1—With a fanfare of brass horns and a telling trombone solo, the lid popped off the Willow Swamp League today and fell into the diamond with a resounding crash. Throughout the land of alfalfa the populace turned baseball-mad and long before daylight the fans were pouring into Bobbletown.

Your correspondent was on the job at the break of day and, with the palpitating throngs, awaited the arrival of the Slug-center Curve Busters. The excitement reached a bursting point when it was observed that the first person who alighted from the hacks was Whitey Whipsaw, the new pitching wonder.

While it was unknown to the general public, those on the inside were fully aware of the new two-handed curve that Whipsaw had developed during the spring while hunting squirrels in Buck Ague's swamp. He had come here today to put a crimp in the batting record of our one and only Swat Mulligan.

The Curve Busters had planned a coup that was to startle the entire baseball world. As is well known, the new rule permits a pitcher to throw as many balls at once as he can conveniently

throw. Whipsaw threw two balls at once, and they crossed before they reached the plate. If the batter missed both balls, it was counted as two strikes. If he repeated he was out, and the pitcher had one strike saved over for the next batter.

The curve was to be the downfall of Swat Mulligan. Everyone was greatly interested, and the gates were open long before game time. At 3 o'clock Mayor Perkins threw out the first ball. But even as the game grew in intensity, Swat could be seen sitting languidly on the bench, smiling calmly.

It might be well to add that Swat's secret service bureau had not been idle. They had investigated, and in Swat's hip pocket was a report of their findings.

In the early innings the Slugcenter boys piled up eight runs, and the Poison Oaks were staring into the face of a row of goose eggs.

In the last half of the seventh, Jerre Linekick, Poison Oak's shortstop, got a base on balls, and Whipsaw walked both Aikens and Sigmun to fill the bases. The psychological moment had arrived. Swat left the bench and started to bat in the place of the Poison Oak pitcher.

Whipsaw smiled sardonically as Mulligan brushed the dust from his bat and took a position at the plate. Whipsaw let loose his famous double-barreled curve.

Pst! Two balls shot past and the umpire yelled, "Two strikes." The crowd groaned.

Just as Whipsaw began to wind up for the next shot a steely glint came into Swat's eyes and he waited for what might come.

As the balls left Whipsaw's hands, Swat saw that they were describing a perfect parabola of about ten degrees. According to his calculations, he figured the balls would cross horizontally six feet and four inches from the plate.

True to Swat's calculations, the balls crossed at the spot indicated. Then Mulligan acted. He jumped six feet out of the batter's box and with a resounding crash hit both balls as they were about to cross. The balls shot forward, one sailing over the right field fence, and the other clearing the left field obstruction by forty feet.

Under the new double-barreled rules the hit counted for two home runs. Every score made thereon counted double. The old rule also was in vogue which permits a batter to score as many runs as he can before the ball is recovered. With a triumphant chuckle Mulligan sped around the bases 98 times. That gave him a total of 196 runs in addition to those scored by the three runners on the bases. That being enough to hold Slugcenter for a while, Swat calmly resumed his position on the bench and watched the P.O. pitcher strike out the rest of the Curve Buster batters. Tonight the town is lighted by bonfires and the populace is crazy with joy.

Score:									*Total*
Slugcenters 0	4	2	0	2	0	0	0	0	8
Poison Oaks 0	0	0	0	0	0	199	0	0	199

Batteries—Whipsaw and Holdcramp; Rapidfire and Tarre.
Attendance, 1,682.

IV

PUNCH LINES

TESTY-MONIAL

George Raft helped Maxie Rosenbloom up the ladder to the light-heavyweight crown, and when the Friars Club threw Raft a testimonial dinner to celebrate Raft's 25th year in pictures, Maxie was on hand as one of the speakers.

"Gents," roared the irrepressible Maxie to the biggest names in movie making, "I owe a lot to George Raft. When I first met da bum, I din't have two bits to my name. Now I owe $25,000. T'anks, Georgie."

THE LORD HASN'T A PRAYER

The fabulous fighter, Ray Robinson, is an odd paradox. One minute after putting the financial screws on a promoter, firing a couple of managers, or trying to milk nickels out of a block of concrete, he'll send up a cloud of piety about how much he owes the Lord, how the good Lord is always watching over him, etc. This was particularly true before his fight with Basilio.

"The way Ray was talking," a reporter said, "I figured he had gone into business with the Lord."

"If he has," remarked a cynical manager, "you can bet that the Lord will be only vice president of the company."

COUNT TO TEN

The boxer was jolted to the canvas. Though he didn't seem to be hit very hard, he rose just too late to beat the 10 count.

"What happened to you?" bellowed his manager. "You weren't really hurt. Why didn't you get up faster?"

"No, I wasn't hurt," explained the boxer. "But I was so mad about being flattened by that punk that I decided to count to 10 before I did anything."

FIST COME, FIST SERVED

The third-rate fighter was getting his lumps and being none-too-happy about the whole affair.

"Stop those punches!" bellowed his angry manager from the corner.

Through battered lips, the fighter wheezed, "You don't see any of them gettin' past me, do you?"

DOWN MEMORY LANE

The boxer went to a doctor because his memory was failing. The medicine man told him not to worry. With about two years of weekly treatment, his memory would return as good as ever. Sure enough, two years later the boxer was discharged with his memory completely restored.

Bouncing happily out of the office, the boxer ran into a man who stuck his hand out. "How are you, Pete," he said.

"Don't tell me your name," the fighter quickly answered, snapping his fingers. "I've got it. You're Spider Webster. I fought you in Chicago on June 21, 1948. You weighed 178 pounds, wore white trunks with a black stripe, and had a red bathrobe with 'Kelly's Gym' on the back. Right?" he chortled.

"Pete, Pete," replied the other. "Don't you remember me? I'm your brother, Harry."

BAER FACTS OF LIFE

While training in New York, Ingemar Johansson was visited by the ex-champ, Max Baer, whose penchant for night life cut short his boxing career—much to his relief. Maxie cornered the champ and quipped:

"Kid, no matter how long you hold the title, you'll never

be able to match my record. I was the only fighter who ever lived who could predict the round in which he'd lose."

Maxie then offered a parting word of advice: "If you ever get belted and see three fighters through a haze, go after the one in the middle. That's what ruined me—I went after the two guys on the end."

RESIN BREAD

Rocky Graziano, former middleweight champ, was stopped by a fight fan who mentioned that he had once seen Graziano knocked down in a bout.

"Which time?" Rocky asked. "I got so much resin in me from knockdowns that whenever I pass Carnegie Hall the violins stand at attention."

TUNNEY-FISH SANDWICH

When Gene Tunney was training for his first fight with Jack Dempsey, people laughed at stories of Tunney reading Shakespeare. A young reporter cornered Gene one afternoon and asked if he (Tunney) had ever written anything himself.

The Fighting Marine snapped, "No! Enough people are laughing at me because I can read. Imagine what they'd do if they thought I could write, too."

BIG BAD BAER

Max Baer blew into New York for a TV show, and was asked to pose for a publicity photo. Because the ex-champ dwarfed the other members in the cast, he was asked to kneel in front of the group. As he went down on one knee, he remarked:

"The last time I was in this position, I was in Madison Square Garden and got $200,000 for it!"

MONGOOSE FOR THE GANDER

Before the Patterson-Moore imbroglio, an esthetic sportswriter wrote that Patterson has "the venomous striking speed of a cobra." Advised of this literary turn, Moore neatly rounded out the metaphor with "And I am a mongoose." Then Patterson neatly rounded out Archie.

WHAT A SPOT

Joe Louis's wartime buddy was Porky Oliver, the jocular golf pro. Most of their duties consisted of daily reconnaissance on the links. After a couple of weeks, Porky had Joe separated from several thousand dollars.

Next time they met on the course, the heavyweight champ quietly announced, "We're playing double or nothing and you're giving me four shots as a spot." Porky protested it wasn't fair. Responded Joe, pointing to his sergeant's chevrons, "Well, I'm pulling rank."

After collecting his money at the end of the day, Louis was stricken by conscience. "Tell you what," he said, draping his arm around Porky, "I'll give you a chance to get even. Let's go up to the gym and box four rounds. I'll spot you the first two."

POSITION IN LIFE

After being knocked out by Ingemar Johansson, Floyd Patterson brooded in a darkened room for days. Finally he went out for a walk, and when he came home he had a joke to tell.

"I walked around and nobody knew me. Then I sat down on a bench—and in that position everybody recognized me."

CLOCK WATCHER

Knocked down for the ninth time in the fight, the battered boxer looked all but out. From the corner his excited manager yelled, "Stay down until eight!"

Lifting his head from the canvas, the fighter wearily asked, "What time is it now?"

V

TEE-HEES AND HAWS

ROCKS IN HIS HEAD

Playing with a duffer buddy, Sammy Snead kept driving the ball out of sight. Each time they'd stroll down the fairway and find the balls about 45 yards apart. And each time Sammy would explain, "I guess I hit a rock and bounced."

On the fifth hole, the balls were 60 yards apart. "Who's that?" asked the duffer pointing to the first ball.

"That's me," said Snead. "I guess I hit a rock and bounced."

"What the hell are you doing, Snead?" roared the duffer, flinging his club in the air, "Aiming at those damn rocks?"

MOURNING DATE

Jimmy Demaret had just lost to Ben Hogan by 10 and 9 in the PGA tournament, and a reporter asked him what he considered the turning point in the match.

"It must have been about 10 o'clock this morning," replied Demaret, "when Ben showed up for the match."

SMALL TALK

Jimmy Demaret scouts the opinion that Ben Hogan is a sulking, uncommunicative opponent on the golf course.

"Ben talks to me on every green," jaunty Jimmy insists. "But he always says the same thing: 'You're away.' "

IT'S A LIE!

All the inept duffer had to do to break 125 for the first time was to sink a 1-foot putt. Ashen with excitement, he crawled around the green for 10 minutes studying the lie. He studied every blade of grass, carefully tested the wind. Then he turned to his caddie.

"How should I play this putt, son?" he appealed.

"Keep it low," cracked the amused cynic.

GO CHASE YOURSELF!

The country club's most fanatical golfer toured the course one morning with a fellow pulling a chaise longue behind him.

"What's the idea?" asked a friend. "Why is your caddie dragging that couch all over the course?"

"Caddie, my foot!" snapped the golfer. "That's my psychiatrist!"

LOST IN THE ROUGH

The two male golfers went berserk playing behind a pair of dilatory female duffers. The gals stopped to chat, picked flowers, admired the scenery, while the poor fellows behind them raged and fumed.

At one point, the two men stood on the tee for nearly 25 minutes while one of the women apparently looked for her ball a few yards down the fairway.

"Why don't you help your friend find her ball?" yelled one of the men to the second woman who stood watching her companion search.

"Oh, she's got her ball," the woman replied sweetly. "She's looking for her club."

PUTT AND TAKE

Passing thoughts on the humbling game of golf:

Golf is a lot of walking, broken up by disappointment and bad arithmetic.

A golfer is a guy who can walk several miles toting 100

pounds of equipment, but who has Junior bring him an ash tray.

Golf is like taxes; you drive hard to make the green and then wind up in the hole.

To put is to place a thing where you want it. To putt is a vain attempt to do the same thing.

BOOKKEEPING WORM

The business tycoon was advising his son's tutor, "There's no sense in teaching the boy to count over 100. He can hire accountants to do his bookkeeping."

"You're right, sir," retorted the tutor. "But he'll want to play his own game of golf, won't he?"

HAVE A STROKE

At a golf tournament recently, the club chairman was surprised to catch the local minister driving off about 10 yards in front of the tee mark.

"I'm afraid, sir," he remarked, "you must be disqualified. You just can't do that."

"Can't do what?" demanded the reverend indignantly.

"Why, drive off from the ladies' tee."

"My friend," the pastor murmured, "I'm playing my *third* stroke."

THE LONG BALL

Columbia's affable football coach, Buff Donelli, was talking about golf. "I played the game a bit when I was younger. Wasn't any star, but hit the long ball occasionally." Turning to his wife for confirmation, he said, "I could hit the long ball, couldn't I, dear?"

"Yes, Buff," she replied. "It was the small white ball that gave you trouble."

IT'S NOT BANANA OIL

Playing over a drought-stricken course in Odessa, Texas, Tommy Bolt became annoyed. "With all the money in Texas," he informed the club manager, "why haven't you been able to get some grass on this course?"

The manager shrugged. "We spent $70,000 last year on an irrigation system, but the only thing that comes up is oil."

HIGH, WIDE AND HANDSOME

Charley Boswell, the blind golfing champ, was playing a friendly match in a foursome and was hooking or slicing all over the course. As his partner lined him up for a tee shot at a climactic stage in the match, Boswell asked what was the distance of the hole.

"You don't have to worry about length," replied his partner. "It's the *width* you've got to think about."

CAR PORT

A couple of movie tycoons decided to take up golf. They purchased all the essential equipment and had their chauffeurs drop them at the nearby country club. There they were informed that they couldn't play that afternoon.

"Why not?" they demanded indignantly.

"Because," the starter informed them, "there are no caddies."

The producers looked at each other for a moment. Then one said, "So who cares? For one afternoon we'll take a Buick."

SPOON FED

Playing golf while on vacation in Scotland, the American duffer called for his No. 5 iron. "Against this wind," observed his caddie, "yon's a spoon shot."

"Nonsense," snapped the golfer, "give me my No. 5." The caddie shook his head and persisted, "Tak' ma tip an' tak' yer spoon."

The American snatched his No. 5 from the bag, lined up his shot, and let go. The ball rose, hit the green, and rolled lazily toward the hole—and fell in!

"Well," he cried, "how about that!"

"Na'sae bad," replied the caddie unperturbably, "but ye'd have done it be'er wi' a spoon!"

BRIDE BRIBE

"Golf! Golf!" snarled the little woman. "I really believe I'd drop dead if you spent one Sunday at home." Hubby sighed. "Now, now, it's no use talking like that. You know you can't bribe me."

VI

TO WIT

THIS WILL KILL YOU

The second-rate surgeon returned from a hunting trip empty-handed. "I didn't kill a thing today," he snarled to his spouse.

"Why, that's the first time that's happened in years," replied his unsympathetic wife.

A DOG'S LIFE

The hunting neophytes returned to camp after an all-day session in the woods. One limped in with his shoulder in a sling, another was nursing a superficial wound in his leg, a third had a bandage on his ear.

"Don't let it get you down," a veteran hunter cheered. "Anyway, that bulge in your bag shows you're not coming back empty-handed."

The fellow carrying the bag answered wearily, "That bulge is our hunting dog!"

LANGUAGE OF LOVE

Our favorite hunting cartoon shows a fat lady hunter with a smoking rifle in her hands and a look of glee on her face. "I must have hit something," she's exulting. "Just listen to that language!"

FOOD FOR THOUGHT

A trio of big game hunters were resting by their campfire after a tough day on safari. One of them finally announced, "I feel kinda restless. Guess I'll walk before chow."

Several hours later, one of the remaining hunters glanced at his watch. "Gosh," he said, "I wonder what's eating Old Oscar?"

NIGHT-MARE

A horse lover bought a broken-down old mare, and ran into immediate heartache. When he went to the paddock to examine it, he found two veterinarians by its side.

"Is my horse sick?" he asked in dismay.

"Not too badly," they said. "We hope to pull her through."

"But will I be able to race her?" asked the owner.

"Most assuredly," replied one of the vets, "and probably beat her, too!"

BARGAIN BASEMENT

The hot-rodder arrived at the pearly gates in his souped-up car. "You're sure welcome," St. Peter told him, "but we don't allow cars up here."

"Then I'm in the wrong place," declared the hot rodder. "I'm going to try the basement."

Satan welcomed the young man. "Glad to have you," he chortled.

"Good," replied the hot rodder. "Gimme a map of your highways."

"Sorry," said Satan, "we have no roads down here. That's the Hell of it!"

NOTHING BUT A HOUND DOG

The hunting party had been asked to bring only male hounds. One poor fellow, however, had nothing but a female, but because of his needy circumstances he was permitted to include her.

The pack was sent off and in just a matter of seconds was out of sight. The worried hunters stopped to question a nearby farmer. "Did you see some hounds go by?"

"Yep," quoth the fellow.

"See where they went?"

"Nope, but it was the first time I ever seen a fox runnin' fifth!"

ONE BORN EVERY MINUTE

A couple of fishing-tackle salesmen were comparing notes. The first produced a gaudy plug, shiny with all the colors of the rainbow.

"Do you sell many of those?" asked the other. "I can't see a bass ever going for such an awful contraption."

"I don't sell 'em to the bass," replied the other with a grin. "Just to the suckers."

OH SAY CAN YOU SEA

In the Sahara Desert, two travellers stopped their jeep beside a man who was running along in a swim suit.

"I'm on my way to have a swim," the fellow explained.

"But the sea is more than 500 miles away!" exclaimed one of the travellers.

"500 miles away!" murmured the bather. "I say, what a splendid beach!"

A LOT OF BULL

Joe Garagiola was showing his announcing partner, Harry Caray, around his recreation room. Noticing a mounted deer's head above the fireplace, Caray remarked, "I didn't know you were a big game hunter, Joe."

The former Cardinal catcher explained that he hadn't shot the deer, that it had been presented to him by an organization for whom he had made an after-dinner speech.

"You know," said Caray, "you're probably the first guy who ever shot the bull and got a deer."

BOUNCING BOWLER

A noisy patron in the bowling alley's cocktail lounge was given the heave-o three times. Each time he brushed himself off and staggered back.

A league bowler watched the exhibition with interest. Finally he tapped the bouncer on the shoulder.

"You know why that guy keeps coming back?" he said. "You're putting too much backspin on him."

SLOW MOTION

George Eastment, the Manhattan College coach, watched one of his hopeless distance men running the mile. "That boy is so slow," he remarked to a reporter, "that if he ever got caught in the rain, he'd rust to death."

DRINK TO ME ONLY

After a hectic season, the demon sports publicity man went on a safari in the Dark Continent. One day he was captured by cannibals and trussed up in a mud hut. Each day the natives would cut his arm and drink his blood.

Finally he called for the king of the tribe. "You can kill me and eat me if you so desire," he said indignantly. "But I'm sick and tired of getting stuck for the drinks."

WHITE ELEPHANT

Left hook by Shirley Povich, crack columnist for *The Washington Post:* "In demanding a stadium that could seat 100,000 for the Olympics, the Recreation people may be forgetting that America only gets the Olympics every 36 years, if it is lucky. Anyway, a stadium with 100,000 seats is strictly for the Prince of Nashipur, who collects white elephants."

BABES IN THE WOODS

A couple of hunters had been out in the wood for five hours and one of them became panicky. "We're lost!" he cried. "What on earth are we going to do?"

"Take it easy," replied his friend. "All we got to do is shoot an extra deer and the game warden will be here in a minute and a half."

FREEDOM OF WORSHIP

Who said the Russians are atheists? At the Olympic Games, a sportswriter went into the Russian dressing room to see a Soviet runner. All he found was the track coach.

"What time will Rokoff be here?" he asked.

The coach shrugged his shoulders. "Only God knows."

ANIMAL KINGDOM

The confirmed city dweller took his young son to the state fair where he pointed out the champion bulls, champion pigs, champion sheep, champion chickens, etc. Then he asked, "Any questions, son?"

"Yes, Dad," replied Junior. "Who did they have to fight to become champions?"

PIN-POINT MARKSMANSHIP

Sportswriter Leonard Schechter: "Columbia had such a poor team last year they couldn't even win a toss."

Pitcher Tommy Byrne: "The Yankees are going to have a lot of trouble signing me this year—I'm thinking of retiring."

Humorist Abe Burrows: "It isn't as if we're losing a baseball team in Brooklyn as much as we're gaining a parking lot.

NOUVEAU RICHE

Our favorite nephew, Pete, aged 13, was recently taken to his first horse race. Before the meeting got underway, his daddy told him that he was going to place a two-dollar bet for him. He rattled off the names of the horses and Pete picked one. You guessed it. The horse came in and Daddy delivered the winnings to the awed kid.

"Well, Pete," said Dad, "would you like to place a bet on the second race?"

Pete waxed indignant. "Bet with *my* money," he snorted. "No, sir!"

RUSSIAN ROULETTE

The teacher at Lenin High School, Moscow, Russia (state champs in red-herring throwing) inquired about an absentee.

"Oh, Nicholai was banged up playing handball yesterday," explained a classmate.

"Hurt by a ball?" exclaimed the teacher.

"Oh, we weren't using a ball," scornfully replied the pupil. "We were using a hand grenade."

MICKEY MOOSE

The famous Scotch hunter, on a visit to Washington, noticed the mounted head of a bull moose hanging over the fireside of the house at which he was staying. "What sort of an animal is that?" he asked.

"Oh, that's a moose," was the reply.

"A moose!" exclaimed the Scot. "Good heavens, what are your rats like over here?"

A POOL OF FAITH

"Undying faith" could be the label for this one. During tryouts for the varsity swimming team at Bayard Junior High in Wilmington, Delaware, Coach Charles Perrone set up the kids in five lanes and had them dive off at the sound of his gun.

To his amazement, only four broke to the surface. The coach promptly took a dip of his own (with whistle, stopwatch, and sweatshirt). He lifted out a floundering form and checked to see that the kid was okay, then snapped: "How come you dived into the water without knowing how to swim?"

"I knew you wouldn't let me down, Coach!" the kid replied.

GRAPPLING IRON

A burglar entered the town rectory and stumbled into the room of a sleeping priest, who happened to be a former intercollegiate wrestling champ. The burglar's flash awakened the Father who jumped up, wrestled the bandit to the floor, and held him until the police arrived.

Next morning an elderly woman showed up at the rectory to learn if the priest had been harmed. "I read about the robbery in the papers," she explained. "It said you took the crook by throwing a half-nelson at him."

"That's true," smiled the priest.

"Thanks be to God, Father, that you were lucky enough to have one in the room with you."

JOCKEYING FOR POSITION

A horseplayer was complaining about a bet he'd lost and said he suspected that the jockey had pulled the horse to keep it from winning. One of his listeners scoffed, "How can such a little guy pull back such a big, strong animal?"

"You don't know jockeys," replied the horseplayer. "A good jockey can hold an elephant two feet away from a bale of hay all day long."

SPORT PEUR LE SPORT

The locker-room flunky had been laboring at his jobs for 20 years. He swept the floors, mopped the shower rooms, washed the dirty socks, disinfected the pool, cleaned the lockers, picked up the scrappings in the trainer's room, and put out the garbage. All without complaint—until he came home one evening and bitterly cried to his wife:

"Imagine, the school is starting freshmen and jayvee football this year plus track. That means 120 more pairs of dirty socks to wash every night and all that extra sweeping, mopping, and disinfecting. It isn't fair!"

"Why don't you quit?" his wife asked.

"I'd like to," he sobbed. "But how can I give up sports?"

NYET TIME FOR COMEDY

While waiting for a Kremlin meeting to begin, Dr. Nicholas Nyaradi, former Hungarian Minister of Finance, extracted an American newspaper from his briefcase and began reading. A Russian attache waiting with him asked for part of it.

"Ha!" exclaimed the Russian after a few minutes of silence, "just what we always suspected would happen in capitalistic America!"

Dr. Nyaradi glanced at the headline to which the Russian was pointing: It read: INDIANS MURDER SENATORS!

A MILE FOR AN EGG

The wife of the famous distance runner had broken her stopwatch and had trouble preparing his breakfast. "Ron," she finally called in exasperation, "there's only one way I can time your egg—run out and do the mile."

UPS AND DOWNS

Though Roger Counsil, Southern Illinois U.'s outstanding all-around athlete, was considered too heavy for most of his specialties—diving, trampolining, tumbling, and pole vaulting—he did more than all right, never losing a diving event in 26 dual meets.

"Actually," he remarked, "my only talent is for going up and coming down."

FORMULA FOR SUCCESS

Coaches are now doing quite well financially. There's Coach Earnest Hope, for instance. He started poor at the age of 20 and retired 20 years later with a comfortable fortune of $50,000. He accumulated it through effort, economy, dauntless courage, superlative coaching, and the death of an uncle who left him $49,000.

JUDICIOUS PREPAREDNESS

The worried-looking stranger walked up to the clerk in the

general store and ordered all the rotten eggs and overripe tomatoes in the store.

The clerk grinned, "I bet you're going to the auditorium tonight to hear Coach Jones speak."

"No," the stranger grimaced. "I'm Coach Jones."

LOOK SHARP!

Close shave by **Bob** Addie, sports scribe de luxe: "Now that it has been revealed that the Gillette Safety Razor Co. contributed $136,200 to the Olympic Fund, none of our athletes will dare raise even a mustache."

COACH'S WIFE

By SALLY GARLAND FOULKS

Oh, the life of a coach's wife!
It's bad, it's true, when they lose—
But when they win, you're really in,
And all your kids have shoes!

Oh, the life of a coach's wife!
She eats out at this, and at that,
She listens to speeches, and constantly preaches
School spirit—mostly through her hat!

Oh, the life of a coach's wife!
She knows not to mention a raise,
For the question of money is always a honey,
And it's always the woman who pays!

Oh, the life of a coach's wife!
It's worst from August 'til December.
I've been walking the floors outside locker room doors
Longer than I can remember.

Oh, the life of a coach's wife!
She's afraid to pick up the news
For fear of discovering just what is hovering
O'er her—from the editor's views.

Oh, the life of a coach's wife!
He's gone from sun to sun,
When other men are home, he's just started to roam,
When Alumni arrive, he must run.

Oh, the life of a coach's wife!
For whom smoking's a cardinal sin—
But it's worth this and more, a hundred times o'er,
For the annual chance that they'll win!

ORIGINAL HARD-LUCK GUY

He was one of those guys who couldn't pick a winner.
If he bet on the favorite, the favorite lost. If he bet on the
underdog, the favorite won. He just didn't have the touch.
He was the original ill-starred, unlucky stiff.

One day his buddy—a big-time operator really in the
know—approached him. "Sam," he said, "I got two young
fighters looking for managers. They can't miss making a
million bucks. Give me 10 G's and take your pick. One
guy's name is Rocky Marciano. The other's is Tiger Blatz."
Sam forged over the 10G's and chose—Tiger Blatz.

A couple of years later he again ran into his big-operator
pal. "Sam," the fellow said, "I got two young horses. Either
one is sure to make a pile. Give me 20 G's and you can
have your pick. One is Nashua, the other is Slop Bucket."
Sam dug up the 20 G's and picked—Slop Bucket.

Several years later, Sam was down to his last 10 G's when
he again ran into his buddy. "Sam," his pal enthused, "two
young ball-players are looking for personal agents. Give me
10 G's and I'll see that you get the job. Take your pick—
one is Joe DiMaggio, the other is Stinky Grumble." Sam
dug up the dough and picked—Stinky.

After Stinky was sent back to Peoria, Sam flipped his wig.
He decided to go to Hawaii to forget. He went to the near-
est air terminal and asked for a ticket to Hawaii. The young

lady replied: "Sir, we have two planes leaving today. One is a two-engine job, the other is a four-engine plane. You can have your pick."

"What's the difference?" said Sam. "I'll take the two-engine job." In the middle of the Pacific, the motor started sputtering and suddenly the plane started down. Sam rushed up front. "Mister," he screamed to the pilot, "gimme a parachute!"

The pilot shook his head sadly. "I have just two. One is okay, but the other is punctured. I'll give you your pick." Sam grabbed the one closer to him, strapped it on his back, and jumped. Down and down he went. The parachute refused to open. Just as he was about to hit the water, Sam turned his eyes heaven-ward and moaned:

"St. Francis, please save me!"

No sooner were the words out of his mouth, when a ghostly hand emerged from the deep and caught Sam just before he went under. Then a spectral voice was heard:

"St. Francis of Xavier or St. Francis of Assisi?"

PURPS CARE NOT A FIG
IF IT'S YEAR OF THE PIG

By DAN PARKER (*Reprinted from the N. Y. Daily Mirror*)

In this Year of the Pig you'd expect a Hog Show
But what do they give us, instead? A Dog Show!
No sooner'n the Garden's rid of hogs,
Than I find the place over-run by dogs;
Captured by Pekingese and Chow Chows;
Gone to the old Dalmatian Bow Wows.
So, drooling for journalistic glory,
I sank my canine teeth in the story.
Coming to judgment, a second Daniel,
Disguised as an alta cocker Spaniel,
Mingled with Puliks and Great Pyrenees,
Lay down with the Pugs, came up with fleas.
Leading a dog's life, undeterred,

This is what I saw and heard:
There was Little Miss Bo, a-stealing a peep
At a Bedlington she mistook for her sheep.
A long Guyland miss saying "Leave us linger,
"I'm fas-kinated by this English Spring-ger!"
A group of sad-eyed little Bassets
Showing the judges their various assets.
A handler shouting: "Hey, send for a plumb-ber!
"There seems to be a leak sprung in this Clumb-ber!"
(Maybe I'm stupid and maybe I'm dumb
But tell me what mountains this clumber e'er clumb!)
A Seeing Eye Dog being dunned by his feeder:
"Here is the bill; take me now to your leader!"
There's Lina Basquette from Chalfonte's Honey Hollow,
A gal that two Champions are right proud to follow:
Her 60-time winning Great Dane, Stormi Rudio
And kid sister Marge, star of stage, screen and studio.
The biggest in judging, Doc E. S. Montgomery,
From owners and breeders he stands for no flummery.
A Cairn looking up as if not cairn a damb
For a dame's passing tribute: "What a cute little lamb!"
A gambler exclaiming: "I'm willin' to bet yuh
That pernter and setter cross bring a poinsettia!"
In the terrier section a little Norwich
Was lapping its morning dish of porwich.
The bull terrier section I cut dead
When segregation reared its head.
One class for Colored, one for Whites,
A dastardly affront to Canine Rights!
Let's have no Dog Shows in this nation
That don't adhere to integration.
A pedigreed flea sitting sleek and happy on
The ear of a totally unaware Papillon.
D'yuh suppose that yonder Lhasa Apso
Knows what it's all about? P'raps so!
Welcome to the Australian Terrier!
With terriers, the more there are the merrier.
The Shih Tzu, sought for an interview,
Replying, "Tzu whom are you speaking tzu?"
The St. Bernard when he was ast if
He'd rather be a Saint or mastiff,

Replying: "I don't find it hard, sir,
"Being just a St. Bernard, sir.
"In fact I think the life's sublime
"With brandy handy all the time."
An Irish setter asking: "Thiggin thu
Gaelic, my friend?" of a Kerry Blue,
While a wolfhound from the River Shannon
Is rapt in a column by Jimmy Cannon.
A dog expert toasting with rye on the rocks
An exotic breed called Komonodoroks.
That world engulfed me in a fog—
Why should it happen to a dog?
How do they think up names like these:
Samoyeds, Rottweilers, Schipperkes?
Was a gander caught peeking by police
When they started a breed called Pekin-gese?
And why don't they call toy Doberman Pinschers
By a rhyming name like Pinscher Minschers?
And when the judging is done tonight
Let's find if a dog's bark's worse than his bite?
Are Siberian Huskies Mikoyan's pet cereal?
(He should choke on such capitalistic material!)
Is a Maltese the dog for a man yclept Katz?
Should Schnauzers wear trousers or mink-lined spats?
Are Mexican Hairless Dogdom's peons?
Why are so many poodles Leons?
Would smooth-coated Chihuahuas make better pets
If called to their mess with muted cornets?
Which is preferred by the Welsh Corgis—
Purloined sirloin or fried porgies?
Are Rhodesian Ridgebacks really Boer hounds
And why don't the candy men peddle horehounds?
But here is the question that really puzzled,
For asking it I'll p'raps be muzzled:
"In this Year of the Pig, why give us Sealyham
"When they know darned well it isn't really ham?"

WELCOMED SPEECH

An Olympic record that's equalled every four years was tied
by Vice President Nixon when he officially opened the 1960

Winter Olympics in 15 words from a standing start. As Shirley Povich reports, this record will never be surpassed because a welcoming speech of more than 15 words is considered un-Olympic.

H-EXERCISE

Serving as toastmaster at a yearly sports dinner, that fantastic faddist, Bernarr Macfadden, moaningly announced:

"Gentlemen, for 40 years I haven't missed a day of exercise. Today, for the first time in all those years, I missed my exercise and now I feel terrible."

The next speaker was the famous humorist, Harry Hirschfield. He spoke thusly:

"You've just heard Mr. Macfadden say he missed his exercise for the first time in 40 years and that's why he doesn't feel well tonight. You'd think that with his exercising steadily for 40 years, he'd have enough momentum to carry him along for one day. Now, Mr. Macfadden, I haven't exercised in 40 years and tonight I feel great."

THE COACH'S DILEMMA

By DONALD J. SALLS
Football Coach, Jacksonville (Ala.) State College

IF when the season is over and he goes fishing, he takes his job lightly. If he doesn't take time off, he's a slave driver.

IF he's the first coach on the field, he's an eager beaver. If he's the last coach on the field, he has lost interest. If practice runs well without his presence, he's not needed.

IF he drives a big car, he's putting on the dog. If he uses an old car, he's a penny pincher.

IF he holds many meetings with his coaches, he's in need of new ideas. If he doesn't hold meetings, he's a poor administrator.

IF he spends a lot of time with the alumni, he's afraid of his job. If he doesn't cater to the alumni, he can't win without their support.

IF he spends a lot of time going to coaching clinics, he's not original and can't think for himself. If he doesn't go to coaching clinics, he's old-fashioned and not up to date.

IF he tries to make substitutions during the game, he doesn't trust his assistants. If his assistants make all the substitutions, he's lazy.

IF he tries to have a large staff of assistants, he's an empire builder. If he tries to work with a small staff, he can't handle a large staff.

IF he carries a brief case home at night, he's trying to impress his staff. If he doesn't take any work home, he's guilty of not working around the clock.

IF he's friendly with his players and staff, he's too good-natured for his own good. If he stays by himself and doesn't mix, he's an introvert.

IF he makes decisions quickly, he uses snap judgment. If he's slow to give an answer, he's not a quick thinker.

IF he keeps his name in the papers all the time, he's a publicity seeker. If he never has his name in the paper, he doesn't know how to get publicity.

IF he wins all the time, his recruitment practices are doubtful. If he loses most of the time, he doesn't know how to get the players.

IF he enjoys reading this, he has a sense of humor. If he doesn't enjoy this, he didn't win last fall.

TICKED TACT PTO-MAINE

The Day Our Sports Heroes Really Speak Their Minds!

THE OTHER NIGHT, while tossing fitfully on our pallet, we had a wondrous nightmare. We dreamt that a moratorium had been declared on all the marshmallowed inhibitions and conventions of the sports world, and truth suddenly reigned —and snowed—supreme. In this braised new world, all our sports heroes suddenly started speaking their minds—and the earth trembled. As undignified truth piled on undignified truth, we somnambulistically reached for our bedside tape recorder and attached it to our subconscious mind. And this is what came out.

Big League Baseball Club Owner: When a team finishes sixth for five years in a row, some changes must be made. Since no manager could have done more with the kids and culls on the team, it must be my fault. I'm hereby firing myself.

Losing Fighter: The judges were blind to give me three rounds. I don't think I won one. Do I want to fight that guy again? Are you crazy! The guy can murder me every day in the week.

Football Coach: With all the personnel we have coming back, I don't see how we can lose a game this year. We ought to murder Notre Dame, Oklahoma, Ohio State, Army, and Auburn. Unless you newspaper men are prejudiced, you ought to make us a prohibitive favorite for every game.

Basketball Coach: Sure those guys are unbeaten and out-size us five inches a man. But we'll take 'em by 25 points. Remember, we're playing on our home court and have a couple of "homers" reffing.

Tennis Bum: Who wants to turn pro? With all the dough I'm making in amateur tennis, it'd mean taking a cut in salary. Anyway, I'm really a stiff and couldn't take a set from any pro in the game.

All-American High School Hero: I've finally decided to go to Abnormal U. because they're giving me the best cash deal. They've also promised me I won't have to attend classes, and will have a good pro contract waiting when I graduate.

Highly Touted Miler: If the wind conditions and the track are perfect and someone sets a fast pace for three laps, I figure to run the mile in 4:08. *Four* minutes? You're out of your mind! I simply haven't got it in me.

Game Official: Sure I called that big play wrong. After all,

I was out on the town all night and didn't get a wink of sleep. I was yawning when that play occurred. Besides, I can't see without glasses. Who cares anyhow? What do those coaches expect for 25 bucks?

University President: Of course I know all about the excesses in big-time football. But you know what would happen if I tried to deemphasize our football program: I'd be out in the streets selling football programs.

Spitball Pitcher: Certainly I throw the spitball on every other pitch. I couldn't get anyone out without it. But you gotta catch me doing it before you can hang me.

Publicity Man: Billy "The Bomber" Katsavage is a wife-beater, a pickpocket, and a low-grade moron who maintains a high "F" academic average. He's hated by all the players, coaches and students. He wouldn't last a week in any repsect-able college. But he's a helluva football player and we need him to help pay off the mortgage on the stadium.

Athletic Director: Those fuddy-duddies who form our "Main-line Boosters Club" are a pain in the neck to all of us. They corrupt the kids and undermine our athletic structure. But what the hell—they take good care of our scholarship men and buy a lot of tickets.

Sports Announcer: Folks, this is the dullest game you ever saw. If I were you, I'd switch to another channel and watch one of those old-time movies. Good God, here comes another one of those dreadful beer commercials! Quick, turn your dial!

Nikita Khrushchev: I must confess that Russia didn't invent shuffleboard, skin diving or judo.

WHAT IS A TRACK MAN?

By ERNIE GORR, *Track Coach, University of Omaha*

SOMEWHERE between the crawling stage of a young boy and the walking stage of an old man there is the ambitious individual called a runner, or track man. Track men are as varied as any other athlete or individual. They are tall, short, stocky, skinny, willowy, springy, or strong, and all have a similar desire: to excel by breaking records or force someone else to break records.

THEY DO NOT get all the recognition of a football, basketball, or baseball player, but they still have the courage to continue to run, jump or throw. They know that with more work sometime they will be up there at the top and their efforts will be recognized by others than their coach, or dad and mother.

A TRACK MAN starts slow and finishes fast; or starts too fast and barely finishes. He will jump or throw great distances in one meet and slip to the basement in another. When the competition is tough, he may outdo himself; or when it is weak, he may just perform.

TRACK ATHLETES are composites—they eat as if they're on a diet, or gorge as though they've never been fed. They are future Olympic candidates—the coach hopes.

YOU CAN find track people anywhere. They will be running over hill and dale, cinder, board, and dirt tracks, or on streets and roads. They run, hurdle, jump, throw, and vault at any age. Each time they strive to outdo their own previous efforts or the other fellow's.

HE IS ALWAYS friendly and courteous, and makes friends with his opponents. But in the true American manner, he'll try to beat him. His race, religion, and social position mean nothing, because it's how fast he runs, how far he jumps, or how far he throws that measures him. He's a team man. He performs as an individual, but he's a great team man.

HE PRACTICES harder, works longer, and is bent on bringing recognition to his school. His performance is never a relative sort of value because it's always measured and recorded in black and white. He knows how good he is or isn't but he's always trying to be—a champion.

TRACK MEN like movies of themselves, still pictures of their performances, long trips, short trips, running in nice weather, records, outstanding performances, stop watches, tape measures, and the pleasant feeling of doing something better than they've ever done before. They would rather not run lots of wind sprints, or overdistance running; they aren't much for the wind, rain, or cold, but lying in the sun is a most pleasant experience.

A TRACK MAN is really great—he runs because he loves running, and will work for hours all alone. He may be defeated time and time again, but he keeps on working to be a winner some day. He may not be a champion, but when he performs he hopes that if he can't break the record, he'll make his opponent do so.

INDEX

212